CAMPAIGN · 239

PLATAEA 479 BC

The most glorious victory ever seen

WILLIAM SHEPHERD　　　ILLUSTRATED BY PETER DENNIS

Series editor Marcus Cowper

First published in Great Britain in 2012 by Osprey Publishing,
Midland House, West Way, Botley, Oxford OX2 0PH, UK
43-01 21st Street, Suite 220B, Long Island City, NY 11101, USA
Email: info@ospreypublishing.com

A CIP catalogue record for this book is available from the British Library.

ISBN: 978 1 84908 554 0
PDF e-book ISBN: 978 1 84908 555 7
EPUB e-book ISBN: 978 1 78096 030 2

Editorial by Ilios Publishing Ltd, Oxford, UK (www.iliospublishing.com)
Page layout by The Black Spot
Index by Marie-Pierre Evans
Typeset in Sabon and Myriad Pro
Maps by Bounford.com
3D bird's-eye view by The Black Spot
Battlescene illustrations by Peter Dennis
Originated by Blenheim Colour Ltd.
Printed in China through World Print Ltd.

13 14 15 16   11 10 9 8 7 6 5 4 3

www.ospreypublishing.com

ARTIST'S NOTE

Readers may care to note that the original paintings from which the colour
plates in this book were prepared are available for private sale. The
Publishers retain all reproduction copyright whatsoever. All enquiries
should be addressed to:

Peter Dennis, Fieldhead, The Park, Mansfield, NOTTS, NG18 2AT, UK

magie.h@ntlworld.com

The Publishers regret that they can enter into no correspondence
upon this matter.

AUTHOR'S NOTE

Text references are given for translated extracts from Herodotus and other
ancient sources in the normal fashion. The translations are my own. I have
also given references where my narrative paraphrases or summarizes
substantial pieces of Herodotus. I have used the more comfortable latinized
spellings of Greek and Persian names, in *Oxford Classical Dictionary* style.
     The photographs are my own other than those whose sources are given
in the captions; permission to use these images is gratefully acknowledged.
     My thanks to Paul Cartledge, Richard Field, Jeremy Mynott and Henry
Shepherd, my son, for reading and commenting on the text at various
stages, and to others who have generously shared insights and expertise;
also to Peter Dennis for, once again, time-travelling with such brilliant vision.
     This book is dedicated to Netta, my wife, in gratitude for her
wholehearted support and tolerance while living amongst it and through it.

THE WOODLAND TRUST

Osprey Publishing are supporting the Woodland Trust, the UK's leading
woodland conservation charity, by funding the dedication of trees.

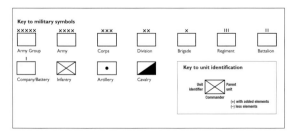

CONTENTS

ORIGINS OF THE CAMPAIGN

Our foremost source begins, 'This *Historia* of Herodotus of Halicarnassus is presented here so that the events of mankind should not fade in memory over time, nor the great and marvellous deeds performed by Hellenes and barbarians go unsung, and, indeed, so that the reason for which they went to war with each other should not be forgotten' (I.1); *Historia* is most accurately translated as 'enquiry' or 'research'. The most usual translation of the word *barbaros* is 'barbarian', but in the early 5th century BC it did not necessarily carry the sense of 'uncivilized' or 'wild'. It was simply applied to anyone 'non-Greek', like the Persians, and the several other peoples that belonged to their empire. The hundreds of independent city-states that called themselves *Hellene* or parts of *Hellas* ('Greek' and 'Greece' are exact translations) differentiated themselves from barbarians by their shared language, shared religion, gods, mythology and certain customs, and their shared ethnic roots (which were actually not much different from the barbarians'). Nothing if not thorough, Herodotus goes deep into the mythical past to identify the original cause of this conflict between Hellenes and barbarians, and traces it back to the war with Troy. In fact, at the time of the Trojan War, the forebears of the Persians were an insignificant people in the midst of the cluster of fabulous civilizations that had existed in the Middle East since the 3rd millennium BC. If the Greek invasion of the Troad offended any superpower, it would have been the Hittites. However, the Persians' Achaemenid Empire, which absorbed those civilizations, was to last over two centuries from 550 BC, when Cyrus the Great conquered the Medes, the Persians' former overlords, until its destruction by Alexander the Great in 330 BC. It was at war with Hellas soon after it came into being.

The Median Empire included half of Assyria (northern Iraq) and Cyrus pushed north from there into Cappadocia (north central Turkey). This empire now bordered the large, militarily powerful and wealthy kingdom of Lydia to the west, a civilization with both Greek and Asian roots. In 547/46 BC, Croesus, king of Lydia, launched an attack on the Persians by crossing the Halys River into Cappadocia. He led his army back to Sardis, the capital of Lydia, after an inconclusive battle at Pteria and disbanded it for the coming winter. At Pteria we simply learn that 'combat was fierce and many fell on each side, ending only when night came with neither side gaining victory'. Croesus did not expect Cyrus to invade Lydia in return because his army had held its own against a considerably larger Persian force. However, he planned to call on his allies to join him in raising a much larger army to take on the Persians again the following year. Cyrus anticipated this strategy, and paying

no respect to the convention of campaigning seasons, marched on Sardis long before it could be put into effect. 'He moved so fast that he himself was the messenger of his own arrival' (I.79). A great battle was fought before the city. Cyrus lined up his camels in front of his infantry and kept his cavalry in the rear. 'As soon as the horses saw and smelled the camels', the Lydian cavalry retreated, but dismounted to fight on foot. 'After many had fallen on each side', the Lydians retreated behind the walls of Sardis and the Persians laid siege to the city. They captured it by sending a force to scale the acropolis at a point where it was supposedly impregnable, having spotted a defender climbing down to recover his helmet, which he had dropped over the side. Croesus had sent urgent messages to his allies, but the siege lasted only two weeks (I.76–84). The Lydians could be described as mounted hoplites, and Herodotus lists them in his catalogue of Xerxes' army as 'armed very much the same as the Greeks' so this appears to have been the first of several victorious encounters with the type of troops that the Persians were to face when they invaded Greece in 480 BC. Herodotus provides frustratingly little information on how the many battles were fought over this period of Persia's growth, but he does give some revealing glimpses of a war machine that was almost invincible in the conquest of Lydia and subsequent campaigns. Persian sources are non-existent.

Cyrus was aware of the Greek city states (*poleis*) spread out along the western coastline of Asia and amongst the islands of the eastern Aegean. These were settlements founded centuries before by Greek migrants from the west. They had mostly flourished individually and quite independently, whilst retaining ties of varying strength with their mother cities in Greece, and some outshone these as powerful centres of wealth and culture. Since the 580s BC they had been uneasy, fairly autonomous and certainly independent-minded subjects of Lydia. As soon as Cyrus had taken control of Sardis, the Ionians informed him of their wish to continue as his subjects on the same long rein and on the same terms as those under which Croesus had ruled them. This was not well received by Cyrus, who had been irritated by their lack of cooperation when he had tried to get them to rebel as a distraction when Croesus was attacking him in Cappadocia. The Ionians asked the Spartans to send military help but they were not willing to do this. Instead they sent a herald to warn Cyrus that they would not tolerate it if he did harm to any Greek city. When he had discovered from advisers who the Spartans were, he scoffed at what he saw as a besetting Greek weakness: 'I have never been afraid of people who set aside a place in the middle of their city to hold meetings, swear false oaths and swindle each other. As I live, these Spartans will have troubles of their own rather than the Ionians' to chatter about' (I.153). Napoleon Bonaparte allegedly ridiculed the British in rather similar terms.

Cyrus put the task of subduing Lydia and Ionia into the ruthlessly capable hands of the Median general Harpagus, and, very early in its existence, the Persian Empire went to war with Hellas. In one interpretation of the hazy chronology of this part of his reign, Cyrus then campaigned far to the east, subduing and bringing into the empire the wide plains and rugged highlands that lay between the Oxus River (Amu Darya) in the north and the Hindu Kush. The mobile and fierce armies of the Sacae and Bactrians were a powerful new asset and a strong buffer against the constantly threatening nomads of the steppes of Central Asia. In 539 BC Cyrus invaded Babylonia (southern Iraq), won what seems to have been an easy victory outside the great city and then laid siege to it. In Herodotus' account, the taking of Babylon highlights the quality of Cyrus' generalship and Persian excellence at siege warfare. According to Herodotus, the Babylonians had carefully prepared for this siege as they observed Cyrus' succession of conquests and confidently awaited him behind their moat and massive double ring of ramparts with a vast stockpile of food. The Euphrates flowed through the centre of the city, in and out of the circle of walls through two openings, which were protected by the depth of the channel and the strength of the current. However, the Persians lowered the water level by diverting the river upstream and took the city in a devastating surprise night-attack by wading in at each end. The bronze gates that sealed off the streets of the city from the riverbanks had been left open and the outer city was overrun whilst those in the centre, oblivious, 'happened to be celebrating a festival, dancing, singing and revelling' (I.190–91). Babylon, the richest and final prize in Cyrus' extraordinary career, completed the amalgamation of the three great, ancient Mesopotamian empires – Assyria, Media and Babylonia – into a single

Lion in glazed brick from 6th-century Babylon. National Museum, Istanbul.

'Man of bronze'; late 6th-century hoplite figurine. Metropolitan Museum of Art, New York.

colossus, which stretched at its peak 6,000km (3,700 miles) from its westernmost points in Thrace and Libya to the river Indus. The conquest of Babylonia brought into the empire Syria, Palestine and, most important for its superb navy, Phoenicia. Sea power would increase Persia's capacity for expansion. In geopolitical terms, after Egypt, Europe was the next logical target. However, in 530 BC Cyrus was drawn east of the Caspian where 'a boundless plain stretches as far as the eye can see. The Massagetae possess the largest share of this great plain and Cyrus decided he wanted to go to war with these people'. After some initial success, the two sides met in 'the most violent battle ever fought between barbarians'. Unfortunately, Herodotus says no more than that a massive exchange of arrows was followed by ferocious close-quarter fighting with spears and short swords. The Persians were heavily defeated, their only major military setback in nearly two decades, and Cyrus was killed.

Cambyses, one of his sons, succeeded Cyrus. In 525 BC, spurned in his attempt to marry into the Egyptian royal family, he carried on his father's mission by going to war against Egypt with a mixed army, including subject Greek levies from Ionia and Aeolis (north of Ionia), and, from an important voluntary newcomer to the empire, Cyprus, previously subject to Egypt. He won a decisive victory at Pelusium on the eastern edge of the Nile delta over an Egyptian army that included Hellene and Carian mercenaries and fielded its own hoplite-style troops. With the subsequent siege and capture of Memphis, 2,500 years and 26 dynasties after its establishment, the kingdom of Egypt became a Persian province. Libya and the important Greek settlement of Cyrene and its neighbours quickly submitted. Cambyses planned a sea campaign against Carthage, but the Phoenician navy refused to take part because settlers from Tyre had founded the city sometime in the 8th century BC. 'So the Carthaginians escaped being enslaved, because Cambyses thought it would not be right to compel the Phoenicians, both because the Phoenicians had submitted to Persia of their own free will, and because Persian seapower was so dependent on them.' (III.7–19)

In 522 BC, Cambyses, now under threat of a coup, died a death that may not have been accidental. He had left no heir and, after some months of civil war, Darius, a distant relation, succeeded him as Great King. He had been one of Cambyses' commanders and was strongly supported by the Persian nucleus of the army. He needed this support in the early months of his reign to suppress rebellion in Media, Babylonia and even Persia, and also further afield, including Armenia and Bactria. Imperial expansion was ruled out for the time being, but, around 518 BC, now confident that his position was secure, he pushed out east to add the valuable province of India (a large part of the Indus basin not the whole subcontinent). However, Darius' main preoccupation at this time was to build on the work of his predecessors to create the extraordinary administrative, financial and governmental infrastructure by means of which he and his successors were to maintain and run their empire for the next two centuries. Important elements survived Alexander's conquest and into the Seleucid era.

A few years later Darius launched the first Persian invasion of Europe. As his son and successor Xerxes would do in 480 BC, he had a bridge of boats built across the Hellespont. His large army rolled over Thrace towards the Istros (Danube), encountering little opposition. The goal, according to Herodotus, was to punish the Scythians for previous aggression against Media, but the strategic objective would have been, as usual, territorial

expansion and the creation of a more deeply buffered frontier. A second bridge of boats was built across the Istros. This was the responsibility of the Ionian Greek levies who had sailed into the Black Sea and up the river in support of the land force. Herodotus describes a massive sweep eastward across the top of the Black Sea, even into the land of the mysterious Black Cloaks and Maneaters, and 'the uninhabited area', with the Persians constantly drawn onwards by the retreating Scythians over scorched earth. Finally Darius decided to retreat. He returned to Persia leaving a force behind in the Chersonese (Gallipoli) under one of his most trusted generals to complete the subjugation of this threshold of Europe. This expedition was not a success, but by no means the disaster that it might have been. The northern flank of any future advance into the west, strategically now the only logical direction, had been secured, and control of both shores of the Hellespont was a worthwhile prize.

The Hellespont around the point bridged by the Persians in 513 and 480 BC.

The next campaign into Europe was inspired by an Ionian Greek, Aristagoras, acting tyrant of Miletus. In 500 BC, under the command of a Persian general, Megabates, and with the full support of Artaphernes, *satrap* (governor) of Lydia, a combined Ionian and Persian naval task force sailed to the rich and powerful central Aegean island of Naxos and laid siege to the city. Unexpectedly the Naxians held out for a number of months and the siege was abandoned. A falling-out between Megabates and the reluctantly subordinate Aristagoras, and consequent lack of cooperation between barbarians and Greeks, could have been factors. Success would have given Aristagoras riches and additional power as ruler of Naxos. For Persia the island would have been a strong forward base for further penetration of Greece. This was a minor setback for Persia, but for Aristagoras it was a life-threatening disaster. His only possible course of action was defection. He stood down as tyrant of Miletus, introduced some democratic institutions and declared independence from the rule of the Great King, persuading fellow tyrants along the western shores of Asia to do the same. This action chimed with a widespread sense of grievance that had recently replaced the past 80 years' pragmatic acceptance of Lydian, then Persian overlordship. The globalizing effect of Persian conquest and expansion had made the larger communities with their significant commercial interests less prosperous and also affected smaller cities' standard of living, and this was resented. And, looking west, there was the heady attraction of Athens' fledgling democracy and its contrast with the autocratic rule of tyrants. The words Herodotus puts into Cyrus' mouth when rebuffing the Spartan delegation that visited him at the time of his conquest of Lydia are perhaps an anachronistic reflection of the Persian attitude to these innovations.

Insurrection and its efficient suppression were, by now, a routine part of Persian imperial rule and, with the sea to the west, and secure Asian satrapies to the east, a rebellious Ionia may have been an irritation, but it was probably not seen as a serious threat. Moreover, the separate Greek communities that it comprised had demonstrated little ability to act in concert or enlist practical outside support. So the rebel attack on Sardis, the capital of Lydia, in 498 BC came as a rude shock to the Persians and they were initially unable to muster a sufficient force to counter it. However, the Greek allies were unable to occupy the city for very long and made no impression on its citadel. A fire was started and spread, destroying the important temple of Cybele and probably other holy places, adding the crime of sacrilege to the crimes of rebellion and aggression committed by Greeks against the Persian Empire. Reinforcements arrived from the east and linked up with the garrison to drive the rebels out of the city. They pursued them to Ephesus on the coast and defeated them in battle there, and the Greek survivors dispersed. Herodotus has very little to say about 'the severe defeat' of Aristagoras' army but gives the impression of a more mobile Persian force catching up with the retreating Greeks. The involvement of a substantial Athenian contingent and a smaller one from Eretria on Euboea was deeply offensive to the Persians. As a matter of record, less than a decade before, the Athenians had come to Artaphernes, *satrap* of Lydia, seeking support in the protection of their newly democratic state against the deposed tyrant Hippias' energetic diplomatic campaign to achieve reinstatement with Spartan backing. The Athenian embassy had 'given earth and water' to the Great King, a serious ritual of submission. Shortly after this, when the Athenians had sent another delegation warning the Persians against listening to the demands of tyrannically inclined exiles, Artaphernes commanded them to reinstate Hippias for their own good. The Athenians

LEFT

Pisistratus' bodyguard armed with cudgels and with cloaks over their left arms for protection in the style of light-armed troops. Metropolitan Museum of Art, New York.

RIGHT

Asian cavalry (probably Amazon) riding down a group of hoplites in broken formation. They carry hoplite shields but are wearing unusual *pilos* helmets with earflaps. National Archaeological Museum, Athens.

had refused and declared themselves to be at war with Persia. The brief Athenian and Eretrian involvement in the Ionian Revolt was an act of war which could not be ignored, and it provided justification for further imperial expansion, if that was needed. However, this initial Persian victory did not prevent the Ionian Revolt (misnamed because it was far more extensive than that) spreading northwards to the Hellespont and southwards into Caria, and south and further east to Cyprus, a possession of especial strategic and economic importance. Caria and Cyprus were more Asian than Greek, so this was now rather more than an irritating uprising at the western edges of the empire, and it took the best part of five years to suppress.

Two years later, the rebelling Ionians defeated the Phoenicians, the cream of the Persian navy off Salamis in Cyprus. However, on land, and on the same day according to Herodotus, the Persians were victorious. They then laid siege to the main cities of the island. Soloi held out longest, five months, until 'the Persians dug a tunnel under the outer wall and took it'. At sea the Phoenicians were clearly outfought and possibly outnumbered. But the Persians probably outnumbered the rebels on land, having come to Cyprus 'with a huge force', and subversion may also have played a part. It was another Persian victory over forces that included heavy infantry described by Herodotus as equipped 'much like the Greeks'. (V.108–16, VII.90)

The Persians also fought major battles against hoplite armies on the Asian mainland. At a place called White Pillars on the Marsyas River, a tributary of the Maeander, the Carian rebel army retreated and allowed the barbarians to cross over, aiming to contain them against this obstacle and drive them into it. However, the Persians under Daurises, who had already won back the eastern side of the Hellespont, outnumbered them and probably outflanked them. They fought, as ever, 'fiercely and for a long time' but were defeated. The survivors fell back to Labraunda in the south. Here the Persians surrounded them in a sacred grove and they were about to surrender when the Milesians and other allies arrived to reinforce them, so they fought again 'and suffered an even heavier defeat'. These two barbarian victories may be

Clashes and confrontations

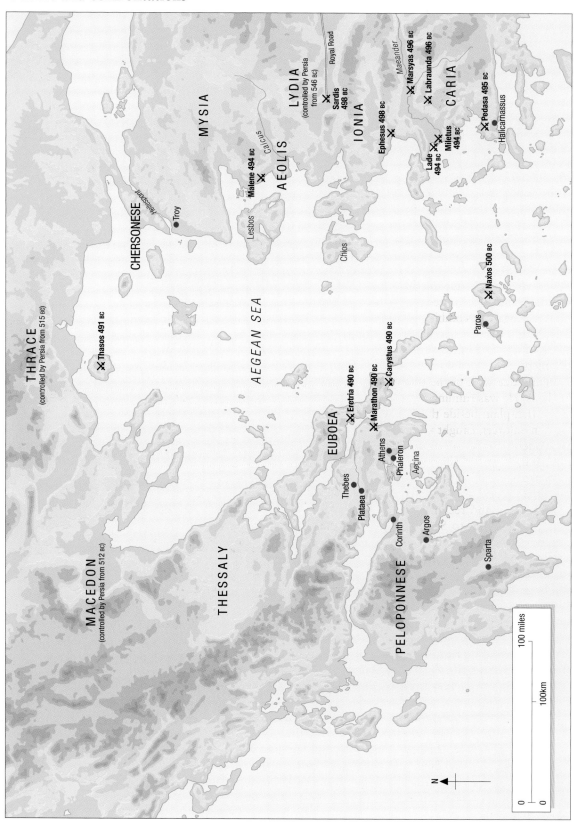

THRACE
(controlled by Persia from 515 BC)

MACEDON
(controlled by Persia from 512 BC)

CHERSONESE

Hellespont

● Troy

MYSIA

Caicus

Malene 494 BC ✕

AEOLIS

Lesbos

Chios

Royal Road

LYDIA
(controlled by Persia from 546 BC)

Maeander

✕ Marsyas 496 BC
✕ Labraunda 496 BC

✕ Sardis
498 BC

IONIA

Ephesus 498 BC ✕

CARIA

✕ Pedasa 495 BC

Lade ✕
494 BC

Miletus
494 BC

✕ Halicarnassus

AEGEAN SEA

✕ Naxos 500 BC

Paros ●

THESSALY

EUBOEA

✕ Eretria 490 BC

✕ Marathon 490 BC
✕ Carystus 490 BC

Athens ●
● Phaleron

Aegina

Thebes ●

Plataea ●

Corinth ●

● Argos

PELOPONNESE

● Sparta

✕ Thasos 491 BC

N

100 miles

100km

0

0

attributed to the Persians' superior mobility and numbers, and, most likely their cavalry, though it is not mentioned. However, they suffered one defeat on land before the Carians were finally subdued. This was at Pedasa, near Halicarnassus, when Daurises and two other generals were killed in a surprise night attack. It may have held up the counterinsurgency campaign for a while.

In 494 BC, with Caria at least contained, the Persians were able to consolidate their forces and march on Miletus, the epicentre of the Revolt. The Milesians prepared to defend their walls whilst a very large Ionian fleet assembled on the island of Lade to counter a seaborne attack. The Persians recognized that they would not be able to capture this strongly fortified port city without command of the sea and took steps to ensure that the rebels did not beat them again. They sent deposed tyrants to offer amnesties to their former subjects, presenting certain defeat and enslavement as the only other option. The alliance held firm initially, but the Samians, who had fought well off Cyprus, decided to accept the terms offered and communicated their intention to desert. So, when the Persians finally attacked, over half the Ionians immediate abandoned the fight, following the lead of 49 out of the 60 Samian ships. The remainder battled heroically, especially the 100-strong Chian fleet, and did a lot of damage to the Persians, but the outcome was inevitable. Now Miletus could be assaulted from the sea as well as the land side, and the city fell. Once again, a combination of subversion and overwhelming force, and, then, highly efficient siegecraft had brought victory. At some point in the final throes of the Ionian Revolt, one of the conspirators, Histiaeus, former tyrant of Miletus, was holding out on Lesbos. He made a foray into Mysia on the mainland due west of the island with a large force of dissident Ionians and Aeolians. He was running out of food and his objective was the grain harvest of the rich plain beside the Caicus River (Bakırçay). Harpagus, the veteran Median enforcer, caught up with them at Malene. According to Herodotus, 'the Greeks stood their ground for a long time… until the cavalry came up and fell upon them. This cavalry action was decisive' (VI.28–29).

When the Persians had put down the Ionian Revolt completely and delivered the retribution they had threatened, they launched a programme of reconciliation and reconstruction. Artaphernes summoned representatives from all the cities to Sardis and imposed regulations to prevent conflict between them, and he had their property boundaries surveyed to prevent disputes and underpin taxation. With Ionia settled, Darius could now reach out further west. He put his nephew and son-in-law, Mardonius, in command of a large army and fleet with the mission of conquering as much of Greece as possible and, specifically, punishing the Athenians for their breach of the oath of submission they had given in 507 BC and their involvement with Eretria in the Ionian Revolt. On his way to the Hellespont, Mardonius reinforced the pacification of Ionia by 'deposing tyrants and establishing democracies in the cities'. Herodotus found this echo of Aristagoras' actions in Miletus in 499 BC 'very surprising', token gesture as it may have been, but it was, of course, in line with present-day counterinsurgency doctrine which states that lasting success is achieved, not by military force, but through political measures. This invasion of 492 BC, actually the third Persian incursion into Europe, extended the Great King's rule from the Hellespont to Macedonia on the mainland, and to the wealthy island of Thasos. However, a lot of ships were lost in a storm off the Athos Peninsula and the expedition ended with a very tough fight with the Brygoi, an aggressive Thracian tribe, which Mardonius was lucky to survive (VI.25–45).

During this decade, Hellas continued to fight her internal wars and Persia would have looked on with keen interest. For example, in 494 BC, Sparta wiped out neighbouring Argos as a serious military force for a generation and consolidated her leadership of the Greeks south of the Isthmus. The deposition and exile of Demaratus, one of their two kings, may have been seen as encouraging evidence of internal instability. Darius made him welcome and he became a trusted adviser to Xerxes, his successor. Athens was continually at war with Aegina, a significant maritime power, and the Persians had subversive links with reactionary factions in Athens through Hippias and his supporters. But the Athenians had also been looking east, uncomfortably aware of the threat that grew as their eastern cousins, the Ionians were progressively subdued. As in Britain in the run-up to World War II, there was a polarizing split between the forces of appeasement, spearheaded by a reactionary rearguard who wanted to turn the political clock back and were even secretly willing to reinstate Hippias, and the forces of resistance. Darius increased the pressure on Greece in 491 BC by commanding subject cities to build warships and transports for an invasion fleet and by dispatching new demands for earth and water to cities that had not yet submitted. The Athenians and Spartans killed the heralds sent to them, an act of extreme sacrilege in both Greek and barbarian eyes. Aegina may have given earth and water as an act of hostility to Athens. Fighting certainly continued between the two cities with losses on both sides and it took Spartan intervention to patch together an uneasy temporary peace. Greece must have seemed a temptingly soft target.

In 490 BC, a large force mustered in Cilicia (south-east Turkey), embarked on the ships assembled there and sailed due west. Datis, a brother of Darius, was in command. Naxos was the first objective in this, the fourth Persian campaign into Europe, and was easily conquered. The Persians fanned out to other islands, levying troops and taking hostages. Carystus at the foot of Euboea put up some opposition before Datis could sweep on to Eretria. Eretria appealed to Athens for assistance. An offer appears to have been made but then withdrawn on discovery of fatal disunity in the city. The Persians disembarked their troops, including the cavalry they had brought with them, and prepared for battle, but the Eretrians would not come out to face them. After a six-day siege the city was betrayed. The Persians destroyed the city and transported the survivors as slaves deep into the Empire. They then made the short crossing to Attica, planning a similar fate for the Athenians. They had met with no naval opposition. Even if the Greeks had been able to assemble a fleet from the relatively small navies of the few cities that might be prepared to bury local rivalries and take the invasion fleet on, the odds would have been impossible. Probably over 300 warships and transports arrived in the long, sheltered bay of Marathon. This was preferred to the Athenian beach at Phaleron because its distance from the city assured an unopposed landing and because the plain beyond was good for cavalry action (VI.95–102).

Approximately 9,000 Athenians with their 600 Plataean allies (and, most likely, a substantial body of light-armed troops) reached the plain of Marathon in time to confront the 15,000–20,000-strong Persian force. Spartan assistance, urgently requested, had not yet arrived. Datis had brought Hippias with him to reinstall as tyrant-governor of Athens. He was now old and sick but still yearning for his former power and homeland. In the several days' stand-off that ensued, the Persians hoped that the now small minority that would have welcomed Hippias back as tyrant would cause division in the defenders' ranks. However, the Athenians held firm and then Miltiades or Callimachus famously

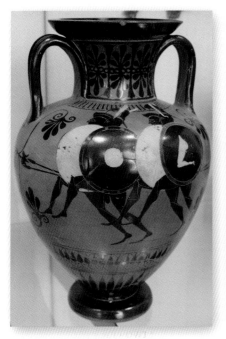

chose his moment to attack. Their stretched centre was driven back and broken, but their right and left, having routed the barbarian flank forces, turned inwards to give Greeks their first-ever land victory over Persians (not counting the Carians' guerrilla triumph five years earlier). Herodotus' account of the battle is very brief but there may be evidence of lessons learned by the hoplite armies of the Ionian Revolt in the timing of the Athenians' attack at a moment when the Persian cavalry could not be involved (possibly away foraging, or back on their transports ready to sail round to Athens), and in their running charge, apparently an innovation, to minimize the effect of the Persian arrow storm. The statement that the Athenians ran a distance of eight *stades* (1,400m) has been widely regarded as heroic inflation. However, this becomes plausible if the pace was a fast walk or a slow trot, and if it is also assumed that the weight of weaponry carried by the hoplites was at the lower end of the estimated range of 15–22kg. Arrows were a threat only over the final 100–150m, which the Greeks would have covered at top speed, most likely losing cohesion on the way. It has been plausibly suggested that the Greeks advanced quickly because they had noticed how long it took the Persians to deploy their cavalry on previous days of the stand-off and timed their charge accordingly (Krentz, 2010). The mythology of this crucial battle must be a significant factor in the recorded total of 6,400 barbarians killed, compared with Athenian losses of 192. In fact, all but seven of the Persian ships were able to get away and Datis felt he still had a strong enough force to take Athens, if he could make it round to Phaleron and land unopposed ahead of the returning Greeks. But their heroic march to block a second landing much closer to the city made the victory decisive. The Spartans, who arrived a couple of days too late for the battle after delaying marching to Athens' aid for sincere religious reasons, were very impressed (VI.103–20). But the mythology built more global significance onto what was unquestionably an outstanding feat of arms than it actually merited. Marathon was not decisive in the way that Salamis and Plataea were decisive and, even if the Persians had won, would the Spartans, Corinthians and others, and indeed the Athenians themselves have allowed Datis to hold onto his prize?

For Darius, Marathon was a modest if embarrassing setback, not a major disaster, though the Athenians certainly enjoyed imagining his rage and frustration. Immediately after the battle or in the following year, Miltiades persuaded the Athenians to carry the war back towards Asia by sending a fleet against Paros, a large island next to Naxos that had surrendered to the Persians without putting up any resistance. The objective was strategic as well as punitive. The island would be valuable as a forward outpost in the Aegean and serve as a base for the recovery of Naxos from Persian rule. However, the expedition failed and Miltiades was seriously wounded and returned to Athens and public disgrace and death from gangrene. For the next eight years Athenians carried on their war with the Aeginetans, who had, along with many others, agreed terms with Persia in the year before Marathon. This conflict between two of the most powerful Greek states was encouraging to the Persians, who expected to exploit such disunity, but they did not anticipate one significant consequence. In the words of Thucydides, writing some 30 years after Herodotus, 'the war with Aegina and the prospect of the barbarian invasion made it possible for Themistocles [the architect of victory at sea in 480 BC] to persuade the Athenians to build the fleet [by far the largest element of the Greek navy] with which they fought at Salamis' (I.14). The absence of any significant mention of Corinth and Sparta in the sources covering this decade suggests that these two major powers were getting on with their lives in reasonable coexistence with the rest of Greece and the outside world.

Darius started planning a new, irresistible invasion soon after Marathon. But then Egypt rebelled and, in 486 BC, he died in the 36th year of his reign. Xerxes, one of his sons and his unchallenged, chosen successor, willingly inherited the mission. But he had to deal with the Egyptians first and then an uprising in Babylonia, two serious disturbances, giving the Greeks six more years' breathing space. The Persians crossed the Hellespont in force for the third time, launching their fifth invasion of Europe in April 480 BC. For detailed accounts of that year's action up to September, see Campaign 188: *Thermopylae 480 BC, Last stand of the 300* (Fields, 2007) and Campaign 222: *Salamis 480 BC, The naval campaign that saved Greece* (Shepherd, 2010).

Herodotus, c.485-425 BC. Without 'the father of history' and his *Enquiry* we would know very little indeed about the war between the Greeks and the Persians. Metropolitan Museum of Art, New York.

CHRONOLOGY

All dates BC

c.1200	Trojan War.
c.557	Cyrus becomes Persian king.
550	Conquest of Media.
546	Conquest of Lydia.
539	Conquest of Babylonia.
530	Death of Cyrus; Cambyses succeeds.
525	Conquest of Egypt.
522	Death of Cambyses, Darius succeeds.
c.518	Conquest of Indus basin.
c.515	First invasion of Europe: conquest of Thrace.
510	Athenians depose the tyrant Hippias; democracy established.
500	Second invasion of Europe; attack on Naxos.
499	Ionian Revolt begins.
498	Burning of Sardis.
494	Battle of Lade and destruction of Miletus; Ionian Revolt ends.
492	Third invasion of Europe: Mardonius' expedition.
490	Fourth invasion of Europe: Datis' invasion of Greece; battle of Marathon.
486	Death of Darius; Xerxes succeeds.
c.485	Birth of Herodotus.
486–85	Suppression of revolts in Egypt and Babylonia.
480	Fifth invasion of Europe.
	August: battles of Artemisium and Thermopylae.
	September: occupation of Attica and Athens.
	Late September: battle of Salamis.
	October: Xerxes returns to Persia; Mardonius winters in Thessaly.
479	June: Mardonius retakes Athens.
	Late July–August: battles of Plataea and Mycale.
478	Campaigns in Cyprus and Hellespont.
	Athens takes over leadership of Hellenic Alliance.
466	Battle of Eurymedon River.
465	Xerxes assassinated; Artaxerxes succeeds.
c.450	Peace treaty between Athens and Persia.
431	Outbreak of Peloponnesian War.
c.425	Death of Herodotus.
424	Death of Artaxerxes; Darius II succeeds.
412	Persian alliance with Sparta.
404	Spartan victory in Peloponnesian War.
387	'The King's Peace'.
330	Alexander's conquest of Persia.

OPPOSING COMMANDERS

PERSIAN

The Persians did not go in for portraits, but this fragment of a relief from Persepolis seems to reflect the qualities they would expect from their leaders, and which were evidently admired by Herodotus in Mardonius. British Museum.

Mardonius was both nephew and son-in-law of Darius and cousin to Xerxes. Herodotus introduces him in 492 BC as the commander of the large army and fleet sent off by the Great King to invade Greece and punish Athens and Eretria for their involvement in the Ionian Revolt. Mardonius had probably been a less senior commander in the suppression of that revolt. He campaigned successfully as far west as Macedonia but then suffered two serious setbacks and, according to Herodotus, returned to Asia in disgrace. Mardonius may have fallen short of his objectives, but 'he didn't leave the Thracians' territory until he had made Persian subjects of them' and he had imposed the Great King's rule over the mainland south of the Black Sea from the Hellespont to Macedonia and the wealthy island of Thasos. However, he was not put in command of the campaign of 490 BC that ended at Marathon. He reappears in 485 BC in Herodotus' narrative driven by 'his love of adventure and desire to be governor of Greece' and successfully urging Xerxes, once he has dealt with revolt in Egypt, to invade Greece and Europe. In 480 BC he was one of the six generals who, as Xerxes' senior staff, shared supreme command of the invading land army. His only recorded involvement in that year's campaigning was to consult the fleet commanders on Xerxes' behalf over what action to take at Salamis. But this is evidence of his close relationship with the Great King and it is probable that he played a central part in the direction of operations throughout.

Herodotus portrays Mardonius as making the case for taking revenge on Athens both as an end in itself and as a warning to others against going to war with Persia, but also has him talking up the beauty and richness of the land of Europe, and scorning the fighting ability of the Greeks. He uses this speech and the response he puts in the mouth of Artabanus, Xerxes' uncle, to illuminate Mardonius' *hubris* (arrogant pride) and anticipate his consequent *nemesis* (fatal retribution). At Plataea, Mardonius' defiance of divine guidance in the shape of the seers' repeated advice not to advance across the Asopus River was a serious act of impiety (which would most likely have been overlooked if it had brought victory) and Herodotus clearly believes this doomed him to his hero's death. He regards Mardonius' decision to retake Athens as driven by 'a terrible lust' and his determination to give battle after ten days' stand-off the consequence of 'folly' and 'lack of judgement'. But both made perfectly good sense. In the former case, the abandonment of their city for a second time and the sight of it burning from Salamis put the Athenians under painful psychological pressure. In the latter, the Greeks had been softened up by days of attrition and were now cut off from their supply line and sources of water. So Herodotus paints a literary portrait of an epic and tragic hero, but within this at the centre of the action is the historic soldier-prince – ambitious, capable and brave – who came very close to setting western civilization on course for a distinctly different future.

Tigranes, commander of the Persian forces in Ionia, was also related to the Great King and, as leader of the Median contingent, had been one of the most senior divisional commanders in the earlier campaign. Herodotus tells us he was the best looking and tallest of the Persians at Mycale, but is probably just following epic convention here. Very little more is known about him. The only other individual who stands out is **Artabazus**, though he makes only a brief appearance in the narrative. He was a cousin of Darius and 'one of the few Persians Xerxes had real respect for'. He held similar rank to Tigranes in Xerxes' invasion army, commanding the Parthian and Chorasmian contingents. After Salamis he was responsible for escorting the Great King back to the Hellespont, and then, on his way to rejoining Mardonius in Thessaly, paused to suppress uprisings in Chalcidice with mixed results. He is presented as a voice of caution amongst Mardonius' staff in the Plataea campaign and, on the final day of the battle, extracted a substantial force to escape the carnage and return safely to Asia.

GREEK

Pausanias, a nephew of Leonidas and regent to his underage son and heir, Pleistarchus, is thought to have been in his mid or late 20s when he took command of the allied land forces. His father, Cleombrotus, would have been regent but he had died in 480 BC after supervising the fortification of the Isthmus of Corinth. Nothing is known of Pausanias' earlier life or specific experience of combat or command, but the cohesion of the Greek alliance under intense pressure can be seen as evidence of considerable powers of leadership, and his conduct of the battle indicates some strategic and tactical instinct, and cool determination. However, inexperience or lack of confidence is suggested by his appointment of another of Leonidas' nephews, **Euryanax**, as a senior aide (IX.10). Herodotus mentions this man only at one other point, supporting Pausanias in the crisis caused by the stubborn Amompharetus during the final night of the battle. Amompharetus could perhaps be seen as a senior veteran, emphatically questioning the young prince's authority. Whatever the exact nature of this crisis, Pausanias steered his command through it, and his leadership may also be credited with the satisfactory resolution of the potentially destructive argument between the Athenians and the Tegeans over their positions in the battleline. Pausanias is shown as paying proper attention to the omens from sacrifice, piously seeking divine support, and receiving it as the battle approaches its climax. He behaves with magnanimity and propriety in victory. Herodotus clearly admires the man, at least for his part in Greece's final victory and for the character he displays in orchestrating it, though he does make references to the subsequent arrogant behaviour which, amongst other factors, swung leadership of the Greek alliance from Sparta to Athens. The sad decade that followed for Pausanias, accused of treason, first for conspiring with Persia and then, at home, for

Sadly, no portrait of Pausanias survives. This early 5th-century bronze statuette depicts a cloaked Spartan warrior with carefully dressed long hair. The transverse crest indicates senior rank. The young regent may have had a less austere appearance if the stories of his later arrogant behaviour are to be believed. But, by Herodotus' account, his conduct of the battle was all that would be expected of a veteran Spartan general. (Wadsworth Museum, Hartford CT)

fomenting rebellion amongst Sparta's Helot underclass, ending with his disgrace and miserable death, is sketched out by Thucydides (I.94–95, 128–34). Herodotus would have approved of Pausanias' later reinstatement as a Spartan hero with statues and a shrine in his honour, shared with Leonidas. The portrait Herodotus builds up artistically contrasts Pausanias with Mardonius, the other main character in *Book IX*, but, as with the latter, a credible image of the historic character also emerges.

Leotychidas, the second of the two Spartan kings, commander-in-chief of the allied fleet and victor of Mycale, is given some background history but stands out as much less of a character than Pausanias in the narrative of the campaign. He was involved in a Spartan intervention in the conflict between Aegina and Athens, which could otherwise have given the Persians a powerful Greek ally within sight of the Acropolis. He had become king in 491 BC in succession to Demaratus. The latter had been deposed in an unsavoury coup, which Leotychidas was part of, and subsequently gone into exile and become a valued adviser in Xerxes' court, accompanying him on campaign in 480 BC. No explanation is given for Pausanias' preferment for the more important command of the Greek land forces, but it doubtless helped to be a nephew of Leonidas, and Leotychidas' more dubious credentials may not have helped his cause. Following the same pattern as Themistocles, the hero of 480 BC, and Pausanias, Leotychidas ended his career under serious accusations of treason. However, the Mycale campaign was quickly and decisively executed and, if the rivalry Herodotus depicts between the Athenians and the Spartans was a significant factor, it appears to have been effectively harnessed.

The generals picked out by Herodotus as commanders of the Athenians at Plataea and Mycale were, respectively, Aristides and Xanthippus. They may have been the most influential generals in their contingents but decision-making was a collective process, depending on a majority vote if necessary. Pausanias' and Leotychidas' supreme authority would have worked in the same way, though both would have been supported by the block vote of the Peloponnesian allies and the traditional respect for Spartan military prowess. **Aristides** is only once and very briefly mentioned by Herodotus in *Book IX*, whereas Plutarch (*c.* AD 50–120), gives him a much more prominent role in his *Life of Aristides*. In part this is a reflection of Plutarch's more biographical and didactic purpose, but he also wished to see the credit for this final and decisive Greek victory more equitably shared across the alliance. Herodotus, for his part, wanted his two main players in *Book IX*, Mardonius and Pausanias, to stand out above all others. It is, at least, clear from his narrative that the Athenians were effectively led and that their interests were well represented in the allied war councils, and Aristides as their top general would have been at the centre of things. But the specific details that Plutarch supplies are generally thought to be pure conjecture, either his own or his Hellenistic predecessors'. However, Aristides was certainly one of the leading politicians of early 5th-century Athens. He was initially one of Themistocles' keenest rivals, but the two of them worked together from late 479 BC in laying the foundations of the Delian League, from which the Athenian Empire grew. **Xanthippus**, a politician of the same 'conservative' hue as Aristides and also a rival of Themistocles in the 480s BC, is best known as the father of Pericles. Like Aristides, he was recalled from ostracism in 481 or 480 BC to play his part in the war effort. After Mycale he campaigned in the Chersonnese, successfully laying siege to Sestus in an exclusively Athenian operation, a precursor of the switch of

leadership from Sparta to Athens in the continuing war against Persia. Herodotus records Aristides' involvement (quite possibly exaggerated or invented) in the battle of Salamis as commander of the force that dealt with the Persians on the island of Psyttaleia. Xanthippus is not mentioned, but would certainly have been there, at least in command of a trireme. Themistocles' absence from the historical record of the campaigns of 479 BC is strange. Perhaps he served under Aristides as a tribal general, or even as a very distinguished citizen hoplite at Plataea, or he was sick and unfit to fight. In any case, his prestige and influence appear to have been as great at the end of 479 BC as at the beginning, so it is unlikely that he temporarily fell out of favour with the people of Athens (as was to happen with permanent effect ten years later).

Hoplites advancing in step and close order, taking the weight of the shield on their left shoulders. The bearded individual appears to be in command. It was normal for generals to fight in the line and lead by example. From the early 4th-century Nereid Monument from Xanthos in Lycia. British Museum.

OPPOSING FORCES

Herodotus explores Xerxes' motivation for the invasion of Greece and his senior commanders' and advisers' attitude to the enemy by recreating a conference at Susa (VII.8–18). Mardonius, the most hawkish contributor to the debate, is fully in favour of the venture and asks:

> What have we to fear? Is it the manpower they can assemble, or the wealth at their disposal? We know how [the Greeks] fight and we know how feeble their resources are. We hold their descendants in our power, those known as Ionians, Aeolians and Dorians, settlers in our land. I have personal experience of these people; I marched against them on your father's orders and reached Macedonia, not far from Athens itself, but none of them came out to fight. Yet, I hear their custom is to declare war on each other and then to go looking for the clearest and most level piece of ground; they make their way there and do battle. The result is, the victors leave the field in a very bad way, but, as for the defeated.... Words fail me! They are completely wiped out. Speaking a common language, as they do, the Greeks ought to make use of heralds and messengers to settle their differences, trying any means other than fighting. But if they have to fight, they should seek out a position that gives least advantage to the other side and offer battle there.

Only Artabanus, Xerxes' uncle, dares to speak against the invasion, warning of the risks and reprimanding Mardonius for underestimating, even slandering the Greeks, 'men who are said to be the best of all at fighting on both land and sea'. Mardonius ultimately wins the argument. His scornful portrayal of the two-centuries-old hoplite method of war, the Greeks' almost ritualistic way of settling disputes between usually neighbouring *poleis* (city states), is accurate as far as it goes. Historically he could point to examples of a preference for fighting defensive battles and lack of tactical imagination.

Earlier, Herodotus puts a Greek view of Persian fighting capability into the mouth of Aristagoras, the Milesian, unsuccessfully seeking support from the Spartan king, Cleomenes, in the liberation of Ionia. 'This is a thing you can easily achieve, for the barbarians are not brave at all, while your fighting qualities are superlative. They go into battle with bows and short spears, wearing trousers and with soft bonnets on their heads' (V.49). A little later, in his successful appeal to the Athenians, Aristagoras adds the information that the Persians fight with neither shield nor spear, the defining gear (*hopla*) of the hoplite, the solid, round *aspis* and the longer, heavier *doru*. However, he makes no mention of the Persians' powerful cavalry arm or of their

A heroically nude hoplite overcomes the Asian enemy, here, as often, depicted as an Amazon. The bow was considered an unmanly weapon, at least by the Spartans. Metropolitan Museum of Art, New York.

prowess at siege warfare and military engineering. It is worth noting that Herodotus later counters Aristagoras' low opinion of the barbarians by praising their bravery in close combat with the more heavily armed Greeks at Thermopylae and Plataea.

Each side actually knew rather more about the other's methods and capabilities than Herodotus suggests. Both had access to handed-down or living memories of almost 70 years of conflict between Greek (or Greek-style) and Asian armies. The former were indeed characterized by relatively static tactics involving close-quarter fighting with heavy infantry, the latter by more fluid

LEFT
This triumphal Attic 'Toby Jug' from the mid-5th century BC is an extraordinary depiction of battlefield stress, and not unsympathetic towards the barbarian. British Museum.

RIGHT
Depictions of barbarians gaining the upper hand are less common, but here the Asian light axe, unusually wielded in the left hand, may be about to prevail over the Greek spear. Metropolitan Museum of Art, New York.

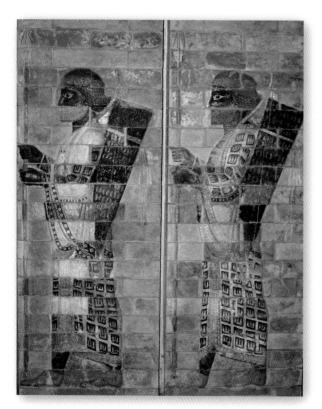

'Immortals' from the elite Great King's Guard in ceremonial dress carrying their bows and large quivers, and spears which were outreached by up to a metre by the hoplite's *doru*. Louvre, Paris.

tactics, fighting at long range with more lightly armed missile troops, on foot or mounted. For decades the Persians had fought against, and sometimes alongside 'men of bronze' (a description of the Carian and Ionian armoured infantry serving the Egyptians in the 7th century BC). They had suffered just one defeat at their hands before Marathon in the exceptional circumstances of the night-time ambush at Pedasa. Marathon, mentioned by Artabanus in Herodotus' debate, had been a defeat of a different order, but it is possible to see how this could have been rationalized as a 'lesson learned'. And before Marathon, the Persians had suffered only one defeat of real significance on land in over 50 years, that at the hands of the Massagetae in 530 BC. Three earlier attacks on Europe, Darius' Scythian adventure in 513 BC, Aristagoras' and Megabates' excursion to Naxos at the turn of the century, and Mardonius' Thracian expedition in 492 BC, had not met all their objectives, but there was good reason to be confident that Persian military might could ultimately achieve full success. At every encounter (except at Pedasa and Marathon) Persian tactics and weaponry, organization and sheer manpower had overcome more heavily armed Greek and other hoplite-style opposition. The Persians had successfully laid siege to stronger and larger cities than any they would come up against in Greece, tunnelling underneath or building great mounds alongside their walls, breaching them with siege engines, or taking the defenders by surprise. They had bridged the Hellespont and the Danube. Intimidation and subversion would play its customary part and their intelligence was good. They knew what forces they would face and had observed decades of internal strife in which the greatest Greek powers were quite regularly at war with each other. They were aware of Sparta's on-off relationship over the years with Athens. Finally, the Persians had given refuge to Hippias, the ousted tyrant and other members of his clan, the Pisistratids, which gave them a direct line to the antidemocratic faction that still existed in Athens. Marathon had proved to be an embarrassing setback at the end of a successful campaign. It had not weakened their belief that they could conquer Greece and had increased their determination to do so.

The Greeks, for their part, were under no illusions about the scale of the threat they were under. Most of the city states decided resistance was hopeless and *medized*, opting for sympathetic neutrality, if not submission and active collaboration. The small number prepared to oppose the invasion, fortunately including some of the greatest military powers in Hellas, recognized, for just as long as it mattered, the desperate importance of cohesion and discipline in the unprecedented alliance that they had formed. The Greek command was able to demonstrate that they understood the relative strengths and weaknesses of the two sides just as well as the Persians did, and proved themselves entirely capable of acting on Mardonius' principle of 'seeking out a position that gives least advantage to the other side'.

PERSIAN FORCES, WEAPONS AND TACTICS

Herodotus comprehensively catalogues the manpower at the Great King's disposal on land and sea in two fascinating lists (VII.60–100). However, out of the 45 peoples itemized, only five feature in his account of Plataea. Xerxes may have included troops from every subject nation in his invasion army, for show and as insurance against insurrection at home, but the main strength came from fewer sources, and significant elements must have remained in Asia to police his provinces and guard the frontiers. After Salamis, Mardonius was given the task of finishing the war in Greece without the support of the navy. He picked out a force that he considered capable of this. The core of it was made up of Persians, including 1,000 Immortals and 1,000 elite cavalry, and Medes, but Herodotus also lists Sacae, Bactrians and Indians, referring to these as 'entire national contingents', altogether a balanced mix of cavalry and infantry. He says Mardonius also chose less numerous representatives from the rest of the army of 480 BC 'selecting them for their looks or in recognition of good service', but, while this may describe Xerxes' criteria, it is unlikely Mardonius bothered with token units. He made a point of including all Persians with body armour (*thorakophoroi*, literally, 'wearing breastplates', but still more lightly armed than Greeks) and added further weight by transferring the heavy-armed Egyptian marines from the fleet. In the following summer he was also able to add to his strength hoplites and heavier cavalry from the medizing states of central and northern Greece. Mardonius was clearly more aware of the tactical challenge presented by the hard hoplite core of the Hellenic Alliance than the words Herodotus puts into his mouth suggest (VIII.113, IX.32).

Mardonius' battle-order at Plataea is not described until the beginning of the middle phase when the two armies took up positions facing each other across the river Asopus. Herodotus mentions only the Persians, the Medes, the Sacae and the medizing Greeks in his account of the actual fighting.

The phalanx concept was not new when the Greeks adopted it in the 7th century BC. This fragment of a grave relief from Lagash, Lower Mesopotamia is dated to 2450 BC and depicts heavy infantry with spears and large shields in close formation. Louvre, Paris.

The Persians wore *tiaras* (soft felt caps), brightly coloured long-sleeved tunics and iron armour which looked like fish scales. Trousers covered their legs and they had *gerra* (wicker shields) rather than proper *aspides* (hoplite shields). They carried their quivers under these and had short spears and long bows with arrows shafted with reeds, and daggers hanging from their belts on their right thighs…. The Medes were similarly equipped. Indeed, this is Median kit, not Persian.
VII.61–62

The *tiara* (or *kurbasa*) was a sort of flapped hood or turban which could be worn open or tied across the face to cover the nose and mouth. Herodotus also uses the word *pilos* and, again, *tiara* for another type of Persian headgear,

looking rather like that worn by Orthodox priests. *Pilos* is also the word for the conical felt, leather or bronze cap worn by hoplites later in the 5th century BC and some elite barbarian troops wore plain bronze helmets, less conical in shape than the Greek *pilos*. The fish-scale tunics may have been the heaviest body armour used, worn only by elite troops. Some Greek vase paintings suggest a kind of quilting which may have incorporated metal plates (an early precursor of the medieval brigandine coat), and others show something similar to the composite cuirasses worn by hoplites from the 6th century BC. But probably the majority wore no body armour at all. The Greeks considered their trousers effeminate. There were two types of shield, the large rectangular *spara*, similar to the medieval pavise, which could be planted in the ground or held up by shieldbearers as protection for archers, and the smaller, more portable variety which was crescent, oval or scalloped in shape. Both were generally made of wicker interwoven with hide strips. Light shields and mobility met the Persians' defensive needs in most of the wars they fought in Asia. The composite bow was their primary weapon with an effective range for its light, reed-shafted arrow of over 100m (300ft) at a high rate of fire. Bow and arrows were carried in a distinctive case, the *gorytos*. In his *Persae*, the tragedy celebrating Athens' glorious victory at Salamis, Aeschylus repeatedly contrasts the bow and the spear, and the bow's symbolic importance in Persian culture is reflected in the depiction of Darius as an archer on the imperial gold and silver coins and in Herodotus' description of his ritualistic shooting of an arrow in the air as he prayed to the gods for vengeance on the Athenians for their part in the attack on Sardis.

Persian and Median cavalry were equipped the same as the infantry, but probably did not carry shields. They were generally sent in to attack first, repeatedly charging up into bowshot and javelin range, harassing, wheeling and retiring. They then made way for the infantry, who continued to shower the enemy with arrows and then attacked with spears, and swords or light axes as secondary weapons; their iron- or bronze-tipped spears were shorter and lighter than the hoplite spear. The cavalry came in again when enemy formations were broken and in flight, riding them down with spears and swords. They were accomplished horsemen, but they rode without stirrups or saddles of any kind, which limited their capability as shock troops, and they could operate effectively only in level, open country on ground that was reasonably kind to unshod hooves. The Persian army was highly organized and, on the Greek side, only the Spartan army was anything like as formally structured. The largest operational unit appears to have had a 'paper strength' of 10,000 and this was made up of ten units of 1,000, which, in turn, were broken down into 100s and tens (*balvarabam*, *hazarabam*, *satabam* and *dathabam*) with a hierarchy of officers for each level. In practice, probably only the 10,000 Immortals maintained this arithmetic exactly, but the structure was a consistent feature. Persians and Medes were highly skilled soldiers, having learned archery and horsemanship from childhood, and they operated within what was, for their times, a sophisticated command structure. They could more appropriately be described as 'professionals' than any of the Greeks except for the Spartans and the small elite units maintained by some other *poleis*.

The Bactrians came from the area of river Oxus (modern Amu) in the north-east of the empire between the Pamir mountains and the Hindu Kush. Their infantry was equipped similarly to the Medes and Persians but with lighter, cane bows. They would not have been so well organized. However,

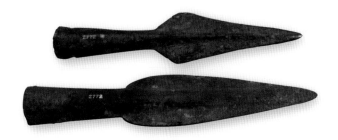

Spearheads, the larger of the two about 20cm (8in.) long. British Museum.

A skin of beaten bronze, typically less than 1mm in thickness, gave further resilience to the shield. The metal was sufficient to turn an edge or a point when struck at an angle but its purpose was more to provide a decorative finish and hold together the woodwork, the main defensive fabric. Willow and poplar (both members of the *salicaceae* family) were preferred for their sappy toughness, which made them resistant to splitting or shattering when pierced or cut. Shields ranged from 80 to 125cm (30–50in.) in diameter and from 4 to 8kg (9–18lb) in weight. Agora Museum, Athens.

their cavalry may have been just as good: it certainly put up tough opposition to Alexander's cavalry in the latter part of the 4th century BC. 'The Indians wore cotton clothing and carried reed bows and iron-tipped reed arrows… their cavalry was dressed and equipped in the same way'. The Sacae (Scythians), cavalry from a little further east of Bactria, were distinguished by their pointed headgear, their own type of bow (the shorter steppes variety) and light battleaxe. The Sacae are singled out by Herodotus as 'the best and the bravest' of the Persian cavalry at Plataea. Along with Persians and Medes, and suggesting they were of similar quality, Sacae foot soldiers were selected to fight as extra marines alongside the native troops of the maritime nations at Artemisium and Salamis. The medizing Greeks were hoplites, presumably with light-armed support, but the Thebans, Thessalians and Macedonians also provided cavalry. These could be classed as medium cavalry, wearing some armour and fighting with javelins that could double as thrusting spears, and swords as a secondary weapon. The Egyptians were the only non-Greeks who were as heavily armed as hoplites with their '"plaited" helmets, broad-rimmed hollow shields, naval pikes, axes, cuirasses and large [falchion-type] swords'. Herodotus picks them out as 'the best of Xerxes' forces at Artemisium', capturing five Greek ships, evidence of their effectiveness in deck-fighting with hoplites. However, in his Plataea order of battle, Herodotus simply describes the Egyptians as 'mingled amongst' the rest, together with 'Phrygians, Thracians, Mysians, Paionians and Ethiopians', and mentions none of these anywhere else in his account. If these nations were represented in Mardonius' army, it seems they did not play a significant part in the fighting.

GREEK FORCES, WEAPONS AND TACTICS

The heavy-armed infantryman known as the hoplite had been an element in the armies of the Greeks for decades before the word *hoplites* appeared in the literature that has come down to us. The archetypal hoplite wore a bronze helmet, body armour (*thorax*) and greaves, and carried a large round shield (*aspis*), a heavy spear (*doru*) and a short sword as a secondary weapon. He is conventionally represented as fighting in a tight, closely ordered *phalanx* formation that was several ranks deep, eight being most usual, with each man occupying a metre of space. The precise mechanics and techniques of hoplite combat have been, and continue to be widely and energetically debated (see, for example, van Wees, 2004, Schwartz, 2010 and Krentz, 2010) but it must be borne in mind that a very large proportion of the written evidence cited dates from the end of the 5th century BC or later, after decades of evolution in fighting methods brought on by the Peloponnesian War. Herodotus uses the word *phalanx* only once and then in its sense of 'log' (of ebony), and he never quantifies the depth of a Greek battle line. Thucydides does not use the word at all, though he notes various file depths. The word occurs quite often in Homer's *Iliad*, but in descriptions of more ancient methods of war, either of the writer's time, the 7th century BC or with some reflection of the 12th century BC, when the war which was his inspiration took place. He uses it in the general sense of 'throng', 'ranks' or 'battle line' without any connotation of the more structured classical hoplite formation. The word's reappearance with a more specialized meaning in 4th-century prose writing may be seen as marking the culmination of an evolutionary process that was still under way at the time of the Persian War, a process that was influenced as much by social and political developments as strategic and tactical. The 'orthodox' view of phalanx combat may well be correct when applied to parochial hoplite-against-hoplite battles. In some of these, a conclusion might be reached and honour satisfied with little bloodshed in a contest that would have seemed to modern eyes to bear more resemblance to a sporting event than warfare. The Persian invasion force with its superior numbers and mobility, and the alien integration of archers and cavalry with light and heavy close-contact infantry presented the Greeks with a rather different set of challenges, including the absence of a shared set of rules.

The shield and the spear were the defining defensive and offensive weapons of the hoplite. Part-time citizen soldiers did not require a high level of drill or training to use them effectively in massed ranks at close quarters. In general, physical fitness from manual labour and exercise in the gymnasium, and readiness to stand by one's kinsmen and neighbours as a matter of honour and civic duty counted for rather more than skill at arms. At this time, the skills of fighting at close quarters with shield, spear and sword were generally regarded as learned by natural instinct. Herodotus does name a number of individuals who were formally or informally voted to have shown most bravery (the verb is *aristeuein*, 'to be the bravest and best') and this suggests that there were phases of combat in which there were opportunities for especially skilled and brave fighters to stand out from the throng, literally as well as metaphorically. The award of distinction (*aristeia*) was also accorded to whole contingents. Formation and manoeuvre do not appear to have been drilled or practised in peacetime by any armies, with the probable exception of the Spartans. At the time of Plataea, hoplite combat was a common-sense way of making war. Depth of file would have been mainly determined by length of front, to keep it at least equal to the enemy's. There seem to have been traditional formulae to settle allied contingents' stations from right to left. Generally the best soldiers, the fittest and best armed, also probably the foremost socially, occupied the front rank. Within units, individuals probably found their positions according to family, local and tribal hierarchy and, once in action, simply had to follow a few basic rules to keep the alignment of ranks and files and to support their comrades in front and to right and left. There was usually little in the way of tactical activity, beyond choosing the place to fight. Battlefield communication was minimal, limited almost entirely to simple trumpet calls signalling advance or retreat.

Butt spikes. Metropolitan Museum of Art, New York.

In a conventional hoplite battle, when the sacrificial omens confirmed that the time had come to fight, the two opposing lines advanced at a walk to maintain cohesion and alignment, perhaps accelerating only in the last few strides before engaging. The lines thudded together, shield against shield, and went to work with their spears till one or the other broke under the pressure of the other side's 'shoving' (*othismos*). What this meant in practical terms is much debated. One interpretation has the front ranks pressed against each other with each man behind pushing his shield into the back of the man in front. Another takes a less literal view, interpreting the word more along the lines of 'thrust' or 'big push' in our contemporary military language. This allows a more open formation and greater scope for individual spear- and swordplay, but does not exclude a lot of pressing of shields on shields. With everyone very closely jammed together, the spear (pointed at both ends) could be used only in overarm thrusts, and striking power with spear or sword would have been greatly reduced by the near-impossibility of moving the feet or pivoting the upper body. And, unless the resistance from the opposing line was completely uniform across its length and depth, the formation would seem likely to become fatally unstable, like a collapsing rugby scrum. However, in some Greek-on-Greek border clashes, combat perhaps was limited to a 'push-of-war', shields against shields, to minimize casualties. In either model, if the broken enemy did not immediately turn and run or call for a truce, the ensuing mêlée would generally quickly become a bloody rout. In broken formation and in flight hoplites became much more vulnerable, and this was the point where the losers' casualties tended to be most severe, as in all ancient and medieval warfare. Mardonius is represented as ridiculing the limitations and simplicity of the hoplite method of war and as questioning the Greeks' ability to adapt to meet the Persian challenge. But it was from this simplicity that Greece drew the strength to resist and finally defeat the world-conquering barbarian invader.

Archer in traditional 'Scythian' dress with exotic, possibly invented headgear. Metropolitan Museum of Art, New York.

Alongside physical fitness and the straightforward code of behaviour, the heavy shield and spear were the only other constants throughout the four-century hoplite era. Up to about halfway through the 5th century BC a hoplite's weapons were his personal possessions, not state-issued; they were his qualification for the role, as was the level of personal wealth they represented. Shields, body armour, helmets and swords, if inherited, were part of a man's wealth. Otherwise he needed to be able to pay the equivalent of many weeks of a craftsman's wage to acquire his kit. Off-the-peg equipment was at the low end of the price range. Made-to-measure helmet, shield and body armour distinguished the richest and most influential from the rest whilst the lowliest might muster with no more than a shield and a spear, perhaps an agricultural knife or cleaver, and a felt or leather cap to provide some head protection. The classic shield was constructed by gluing a number of wooden laths together into a disk and shaping this into its shallow bowl-shape by turning it on a rudimentary lathe. Unfortunately very few examples have survived with any woodwork intact, but the best were probably laminated with the grain running at different angles in successive layers for greater strength. Earlier shields had a central handgrip. The larger kind was supported by a baldric; smaller, lighter shields were held out at arm's length. The greater weight of the hoplite shield was supported by a revolutionary 'double grip' and by resting the upper rim on the left shoulder in sideways fighting stance. This is a strong reason for arguing that hoplites did not literally fight 'shoulder to shoulder', and that it was less important for shields to touch, let alone interlock, than for the arcs covered by each man's spear to overlap with those covered by his two immediate neighbours'.

The hoplite spear (*doru*) was 1.8–2.4m (6–8ft) long. Ash and cornel (a type of dogwood) were preferred for the shaft, which was approximately 2.5cm (1in.) in diameter but tapered a little from the butt. The leaf-shaped head was made of iron, sometimes bronze, and 20–30cm (8–12in.) in length. The butt was tipped with a heavy spike, generally square in section, known as the 'lizard killer' (*sauroter*). The name and square punctures found in some cuirass remains suggest that this may have been used offensively when the head broke off or for conveniently stabbing down on fallen enemies as the phalanx rolled forward. Less dramatically, it served to reinforce the shaft against splitting down its length, counterbalanced the head and added usefully to the weapon's mass; and the spike was useful for sticking the spear upright in the ground. The point of balance, where the spear was held in the right hand for action, was nearer the butt than the tip and bindings of twine or leather to improve grip are depicted in vase paintings. Practical experiments have demonstrated that a thrust delivered overarm was far more powerful than an underarm thrust, but the latter would generally have been aimed at the less well-protected lower half of the body.

The helmets worn by hoplites at Plataea were probably mostly of the iconic 'Corinthian' type. This was impressively crafted from a single beaten and burnished sheet of bronze. The metal, ranging from about 1mm in thickness to 3mm over the brow and nose, and its elegant curvature gave good

This Aeginetan projects steadfast hoplite virtues. The island state of Aegina had been a bitter rival and enemy of her close neighbour, Athens, for years before Xerxes' invasion and had 'given earth and water' to the Persians before Marathon. But their navy made a significant contribution to the Greek victory at Salamis and their forces played their part in the campaigns of 479 BC. Metropolitan Museum of Art, New York.

LEFT
Corinthian helmet. British Museum.

RIGHT
Corinthian helmet. Metropolitan Museum of Art, New York.

protection to the face and skull at the cost of a narrow field of vision, muffled hearing and minimal ventilation. It is often depicted pushed back on top of the head to improve vision and hearing, and provide ventilation when not in close combat. Chest and back were protected by two kinds of body armour, the traditional bronze 'muscle' *thorax* and the more recently developed *linothorax* ('linen breastplate'). The former was much more expensive in terms both of materials and of the craftsmanship involved in working the metal and tailoring it exactly to its owner's measurement. It is clear from the evidence of vase paintings that the *linothorax* was widely used and had begun to supersede the bronze cuirass decades before in the 6th century BC. No remains of the fabric have been found, but there is little doubt that this armour was made by gluing linen in layers. In addition to its relative cheapness and ease of manufacture, the *linothorax* had other important advantages: it would have weighed 3–4kg (7–9lb), around one-third of the weight of the most solid bronze examples; it was cooler to fight in and more comfortable than all but the best-fitting bronze armour; and its flexibility and design allowed one size to be adjusted to fit a reasonable range of body measurements. Some illustrations show examples reinforced with small metal scales or plates. These are generally restricted to the abdominal area suggesting they had a protective as well as a decorative function. However practical experiments using pre-industrial materials have shown that linen alone, glued in layers to a thickness of 12mm, is as resistant to pointed and edged weapons as 2mm bronze plate. A modern reconstruction of a complete *linothorax* working from a basic template did not require a great deal of skill to make. However, although the *linothorax* could be as resilient as the best bronze cuirass and was significantly lighter and much less costly to manufacture, body armour was phased out in Greek armies as the 5th century BC progressed, as was the closed type of helmet, in an evolution comparable to that of tank design with its trade-offs between mobility, protection and striking power.

Herodotus repeatedly states that each hoplite was accompanied by a light-armed soldier (*psilos machimos*), but that the 5,000 Spartans were each 'guarded' by seven Helots, 'all equipped for war'. This demonstrated either surprising trust in the unstable underclass of conquered Messenian serfs on which their society depended or calculation that they would be less of a threat on campaign than left at home. Herodotus hardly mentions the *psiloi* at all in the actual fighting and uses words for them like 'attendant', 'servant' or 'baggage-carrier' reflecting their other support functions. But they undoubtedly had a combat role. There was a separate tomb for Helot casualties at Plataea; the Helot dead at Thermopylae were said to be mistaken for Spartans by the Persians; and Pausanias (the travel writer from the 2nd century AD) mentions a tomb for the Athenian 'slaves' who fought at Marathon, presumably amongst the *psiloi*, just as slaves rowed alongside citizens and resident aliens in the Athenian fleet. Earlier sources (Homer, Tyrtaeus, Archilochus) picture light-armed mingled with heavy-armed and sheltering under their shields in the battle line. At Plataea, the *psiloi* would have included javelin-throwers, slingers and bowmen, and stones were widely used as missiles, though this did not amount to long-range fighting capability that was in any way comparable to the barbarians'. They were most likely used as skirmishers, screening flanks and out in front of the hoplites before the opposing lines engaged. They then fell back to the rear or took shelter in

Bronze cuirass and helmet from the early 5th century BC. Metropolitan Museum of Art, New York.

the line to support the hoplites with missiles, passing forward replacements for broken spears, carrying back the dead and wounded and even plugging gaps with spear and shield (Thucydides records that Helots fought as hoplites, armed by the state, in the Peloponnesian War). Their mobility was an asset in the pursuit of a broken enemy, and Herodotus depicts the Helots gathering up the spoils and stripping the bodies when the battle of Plataea was over. Some of the *psiloi* may have had light shields of wickerwork or hide, others wrapped cloaks or hides around their left arms. Missile 'specialists' probably used hunting weapons for the most part. Some had swords or knives, but more probably wielded farm implements or crude cudgels, and there were always stones lying around. By the Peloponnesian War, light-armed tactics had become more organized and effective, and hoplite equipment became lighter and less elaborate as a counter to this development. Thucydides records several instances in which light-armed units, in support of hoplites or on their own, carried out ambushes, flank attacks or assaults on positions, and defeated hoplite units. Herodotus says very little about their contribution, just as he underplays the contribution of the same social classes, and in 480 BC, the same men, as oarsmen. Slaves and serfs were probably almost as well motivated as the poor free citizens they fought or rowed alongside to defend the way of life which they shared. The Helots were Greeks; slaves were generally non-Greeks.

NUMBERS

Herodotus sets the orders of battle at the beginning of the long middle phase of the confrontation, when the two armies had manoeuvred to face each other across the river Asopus. He gives a total of 350,000 for the Persian army with no indication of how it was divided up between infantry and cavalry, or between contingents, beyond a cautious guess that the medizing Greeks numbered 50,000. However, he is specific about the positions of the main contingents of the Persian army in relation to the Greek contingents opposite them, which gives some idea of their relative strengths. He is rather more precise about the Greeks, although his numbers for the individual contingents do not quite add up to the grand totals he gives of 38,700 hoplites and 69,500 light-armed troops. These numbers can be accepted as based on public record and, in the greatest crisis ever faced by the Greek world, mobilization was probably as near total as it ever would have been. However, they probably reflect total 'paper' strengths and may not properly account for the hoplites and rowers serving in the Greek fleet, or for other unavoidable absences. Nonetheless, a figure in the region of 35,000 seems quite plausible for the hoplite core of Pausanias' army. A good number of the light-armed troops

mustered for the campaign would have been strung out on the long supply route from the Peloponnese but 40,000–50,000 may have been deployed alongside their hoplite superiors or masters on the plain of Plataea. On the Persian side, Mardonius probably did have some numerical advantage but his conduct of the battle strongly suggests that this was not nearly as great as tradition has it, suggesting a total in the region of 100,000 for all the types and races of troops under his command. With a significantly larger force he could have been expected to attempt a decisive move earlier in the confrontation. But this may, in any case, have been ruled out by logistical and manpower considerations. If his army had been closer in size to the Greek army, or smaller than it, then the Greeks would, arguably have been more proactive after they had advanced to the south bank of the Asopus.

Orders of battle (Herodotus IX.28–32)		
Persian	**Greek**	
Various infantry and cavalry	*Hoplite*	*Non-hoplite*
Barbarian Persians	Spartans 5,000 Lacedaemonians 5,000 Tegeans 1,500 Thespians **11,500**	35,000 armed Helots 5,000 1,500 1,800 'survivors'
Medes	Corinthians 5,000 Potidaeans in Corinthian ranks 300 Arcadians of Orchomenus 600 Sicyonians 3,000 **8,900**	5,000 300 600 3,000
Bactrians	Epidaurians 800 Troezenians 1,000 Lepreans 200 Mycenae and Tiryns 400 Phleiasians 1,000 **3,400**	800 1,000 200 400 1,000
Indians	Hermionians 3,000 Eretrians and Styrians 600 Chalcidians 400 **4,000**	3,000 600 400
Sacae TOTAL 300,000	Ambraciots 500 Anactorians and Leucadians 800 Paleans 200 Aeginetans 500 **2,000**	500 800 200 500
Medizing Greeks Hoplites and light-armed from Thebes and Boeotia, Locris, Malis, Macedonia, Thessaly and Phocis TOTAL 50,000	Megarians 3,000 Plataeans 600 Athenians 8,000 **11,600**	3,000 600 8,800 including archers
350,000	41,400	74,000

Mardonius places his best Persian troops opposite the Lacedaemonians and Herodotus tells us that 'they greatly outnumbered them and so were drawn up in greater depth and with their front covering the Tegeans as well'. Pausanias' right-flank division comprised over 10,000 hoplites supported by perhaps twice as many *psiloi* drawn from the 35,000 Helots that Herodotus lists, and the 6,500 he has accompanying the rest of the Lacedaemonians and the Tegeans. The 5,000 Spartans were the military elite from Sparta itself. The 5,000 Lacedaemonians were hoplites from the 80 villages and cities of Lacedaemon, Sparta's autonomous, but dependent and subordinate "neighbours" (*perioikoi*). Spartans could also be correctly described as Lacedaemonians, and Herodotus frequently does so. This division most likely also included 1,800 Thespians, refugees from the destruction of their city after Thermopylae, where 700 of their comrades had stayed to die with Leonidas; Herodotus remarks that they were not fully armed. Taking Herodotus' numbers for the Greeks at absolute face value, Mardonius' Persians 'greatly outnumbered' a massive array of almost 55,000. A figure in the region of 30,000 seems more plausible and makes better sense alongside Herodotus' strength of 24,000 hoplites and light-armed, including an assumed 800 Athenian archers, for the Greek left. So, Mardonius' Persians could be estimated at up to 40,000 (four *balvarabam*). Next in line, his Medes, perhaps 20,000 in two *balvarabam*, faced around 8,000 hoplites and supporting light-armed from the north-eastern Peloponnese, including the powerful cities of Corinth and Sicyon. Then came the Bactrians, Indians and Sacae, perhaps totalling 20,000, up against a number of mostly small contingents from the eastern Peloponnese and Euboea, perhaps 7,500 hoplites in all with an equal number of light-armed.

Mardonius' large force of medizing Greeks from Thebes and further north as far as Macedon, a total of 50,000 hoplites, according to Herodotus' extravagant guess, made up his right flank with light-armed support. The Greek left was anchored by the Athenian hoplites with the 600 faithful Plataeans and 3,000 Megarians to their right, a total of 24,000 if all the light-armed and the Athenian archers were in the line. Athens made the largest contribution to the Greek fleet in the eastern Aegean, so 20,000 seems a better estimate. Thebes and other Boeotian cities, and Locris, Malis and Macedon were capable of fielding a force that was equal to this, and were certainly in enough strength to attack the Greek left and put up a hard fight on the final day of the battle. So, it is likely that the two sides were fairly equally matched here, a larger confrontation of Greek against Greek than any in the Peloponnesian War or the 4th century BC.

The Sacae, Medes, Indians, Bactrians and medizing Greeks also supplied cavalry and, with the 1,000 elite Persian horse that Mardonius retained in Greece at the end of the previous year's campaigning, this important arm would have been several-thousand strong, certainly sufficient to press the Greeks very hard at more than one stage of the battle. It gave the Persians a potential edge over the Greeks; Persian infantry numbers may not have been greatly superior when averaged out along the line, but the Greeks had no cavalry other than a few scouts and dispatch riders. The several hundred Athenian archers were the only substantial counter to the tens of thousands of barbarian mounted and infantry bowmen. The rest of the Greek light-armed troops would have provided no comparable long-range fighting capability.

In the region of 200,000 men fought this battle for the future of western civilization, about the same number as at Waterloo, alive and dead after Blücher had arrived, and rather more than fought at Gettysburg or were shipped over the Channel on D-Day.

OPPOSING PLANS

PERSIAN

The trireme was the capital ship used by both the Greek and Persian navies. The Hellenic Navy's *Olympias* is an extraordinary piece of 'living history'. This full-scale, fully functioning reconstruction was based on scattered fragments of archaeological, sculptural, pictorial and textual evidence, and traditional boatbuilding techniques. (Hellenic Navy)

King Darius had established the absorption of mainland Greece into the Persian Empire as a strategic objective immediately after the Ionian Revolt. The necessary punishment of Athens and Eretria for their involvement would be a part of this operation, but the larger purpose was to create a more stable western frontier and to open up new sources of tribute and military levies; the richer, Greek-occupied territories of Sicily and Southern Italy lay logically and enticingly beyond. On Xerxes' accession, the immediate priority was to restore order in Egypt and Babylonia, and succession doubtless produced other distractions, but Herodotus convincingly depicts the new Great King as very certain of his duty to carry out the mission he has inherited, and as fully understanding its purpose. Xerxes' massive combination of land and sea power for his invasion of Greece was a winning strategy. The Greeks were able to hold the invasion up only for a few days with their own combined-force strategy at Thermopylae and Artemisium, but they did not have the manpower to commit army and navy at full strength simultaneously. If Xerxes had decided simply to contain the Greeks inside the straits of Salamis and to detach a large fleet to outflank the Isthmus defences, the war

could have been over before the winter. Herodotus outlines such a scenario in advice given to Xerxes and, in his narrative of the final day before the battle, he writes 'around nightfall, the barbarian army was on the way towards the Peloponnese', though this may be based on misinterpretation of a less significant troop movement. The fatal decision to enter the straits in force was taken in the expectation that Greek resistance would be no more than patchy and, with the Greek fleet eliminated, the Isthmus position could be easily outflanked by a seaborne force.

The Persian plan for the 479 BC campaign on the Greek mainland did not include naval force, but victory was still a real possibility and would be guaranteed if the Greek alliance could be undermined. This remained a key element of Persian strategy. Overt diplomacy, direct and through intermediaries like Alexander of Macedon, and covert bribery and subversion were the customary tools; even days into the battle of Plataea, Artabazus is presented as advising the Persians not to fight but to buy victory with gold. Mardonius stayed in Attica, doing it no harm and hoping to detach Athens from the Hellenic Alliance, until the Spartans and their allies finally committed to a campaign north of the Isthmus. Then he withdrew into Boeotia, country more suitable for cavalry action. If the war could not be won by other means, the intention was to conclude things by fighting in open, level country where mobility and the reach of missile tactics, and numerical advantage (which was probably not very great) could be exploited to best effect. The Persians fully appreciated the resilience of a tight hoplite formation that maintained its cohesion when under missile attack or engaged at close-quarters by lighter Asian infantry, but they also knew that the advantages of the heavier Greek weaponry evaporated when formations broke. There was also the hope that the Greeks could simply be starved out in a prolonged stand-off at the end of a long and vulnerable supply chain on land that had been stripped bare.

LEFT
2nd-century statue from Samothrace of Nike, goddess of victory, alighting on the prow of a trireme. Louvre, Paris.

RIGHT
3rd-century relief depicting the stern structure of a trireme. Acropolis of Lindos, Rhodes.

At sea, Persia was still able to muster a larger fleet than the Greeks, but a change in strategic thinking, demoralization after Salamis, or priorities elsewhere, or, most likely, a combination of the three, restricted ambition for the campaigning season of 479 BC. However, the reduced fleet that remained in the eastern Aegean, primarily to police Ionia and the Hellespont area, was capable of launching a diversionary attack on the islands or mainland Greece. So its presence diverted significant manpower that would have been very useful to the Greeks at Plataea.

GREEK

The Greeks had been well aware of the growing Persian threat but, for at least a decade, had taken no specific action to prepare to meet it. Then, in 483 BC, under Themistocles' leadership, Athens began the rapid build-up of her navy, without which the war would have been lost in 480 BC. In 479 BC, the Greek objective was simply to resist further penetration of mainland Greece and drive the Persians out by defeating them on land. However, there was the same conflict as in 480 BC between the Peloponnesian view that central Greece should be abandoned and the Persians confronted at the Isthmus, and the Athenian insistence on Boeotia or, later, the Thriasian Plain east of Eleusis as the battleground. The conflict was resolved in the same way, by the Athenians threatening to abandon the Alliance. Herodotus spells out the killer argument dramatically by putting it into the mouth of an otherwise unknown Tegean, 'a foreigner of very great influence in Sparta… saying, "if the Athenians break their bond with us and become allies of the barbarians, however strong a wall you drive across the Isthmus, a great gateway will be opened into the Peloponnese"' (IX.9). Without the Athenians the Alliance's hoplite strength would be reduced by 10,000 and, fatally, its navy would be halved.

It was well understood that victory on land would depend on maintaining cohesion in the face of missile attacks and bringing about circumstances in which hoplites could engage in formation at close quarters and grind down the more numerous but 'softer' barbarian infantry. It was as desirable for the Greeks as for the Persians that the enemy attack them on ground of their choosing, a common situation in ancient battles, which were therefore often preceded by a long stand-off. Both sides needed level and open terrain to

This late 5th-century Athenian relief was the most important piece of evidence for the working of the trireme's three-tier oar system. Acropolis Museum, Athens.

mount an effective attack but barbarian troops required considerably more manoeuvring space, and rising or broken ground added valuably to the strength of a typically static Greek defensive position. At sea, the primary goal was probably to guard against an attack on the western islands or the Greek mainland. However, in the eastern Aegean, as Herodotus grandly puts it, 'the prizes for victory were the islands and the Hellespont'. In any case, renewed instability on the western seaboard of Asia would be a powerful distraction. As far as the Hellespont was concerned, the objective seems to have been free passage rather than absolute control. The placing of a Spartan king in command of the allied fleet may reflect recognition of the importance of the fleet's role and perhaps the intention at some point that it should be larger. However, the Greeks did not sail west from Delos until the Ionians had assured them that they planned to revolt a second time and the Athenian contingent was probably not prepared to move until they knew the Peloponnesians were marching north to join up with the Athenians and the rest of the allies in central Greece. A third factor in the decision may have been intelligence about the Persian fleet's size and condition and, in particular, the Phoenicians' absence from it. The Greeks were apparently prepared to fight a sea-battle, and their success in 480 BC would have given them confidence here, or to land troops to fight on shore. The latter may have seemed more risky, but they would have had good information on the barbarians' numbers and location from the Ionians, who had also assured them of their support, and a land battle would have been more to Leotychidas' taste.

THE CAMPAIGN TO PLATAEA AND MYCALE

After Salamis, the Greeks expected to have to fight again the next day. The Persians, with the uncommitted Egyptian squadron as a nucleus, still had numbers in their favour. However, the crews that had escaped from the straits were demoralized and exhausted, and many of the ships would need work to make them battleworthy again. Xerxes had taken and destroyed Athens and become master of central and northern Greece, and, though he had lost a sea battle, his massive army was intact and undefeated. However, he was a long way from home and the centre of empire, and the campaigning season was drawing to a close.

After some debate, Xerxes took the decision to retreat. The fleet left Phaleron under cover of darkness soon after the battle. At least part of it spent the winter on Samos and this is where it assembled again the following spring. Samos was a good base from which to keep Ionia subdued. The army set off from Attica a few days later. Having reached Thessaly, it divided with most of it remaining in northern Greece under the command of Mardonius with orders to resume hostilities the following spring. At this time, the Spartans were instructed by the Delphic oracle to demand compensation for the death of their king at Thermopylae. They sent a herald to deliver this message to Xerxes. As Herodotus tells it, with obvious relish, 'Xerxes laughed and gave no answer for some time, then pointed to Mardonius, who happened to be

The straits of Salamis from the west. Modern port installations have encroached and the road that runs along the base of them roughly marks the 5th-century shoreline which was at the backs of the Persian ships that faced the Greeks in the late-September dawn the year before Plataea. Greek victory at Salamis ensured the survival of Greece to fight the decisive battle in 479 BC.

Movement of forces

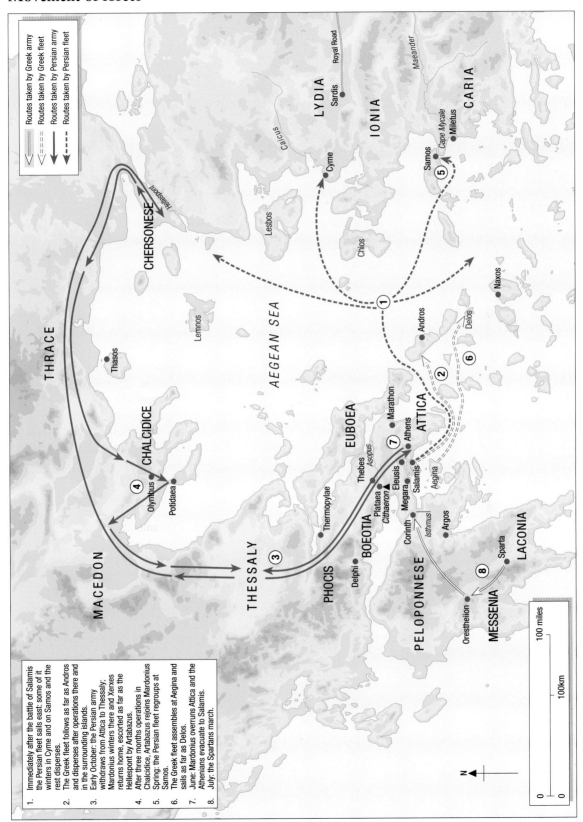

Legend:
- Routes taken by Greek army
- Routes taken by Greek fleet
- Routes taken by Persian army
- Routes taken by Persian fleet

Map labels:

Royal Road, Maeander, LYDIA, IONIA, CARIA, Sardis, Cyme, Cape Mycale, Miletus, Samos (5), Calicus, Lesbos, Chios, Naxos, Andros, Delos, Thracian Hellespont, CHERSONESE, AEGEAN SEA, Lemnos, Thasos, THRACE, CHALCIDICE, Olynthus, Potidaea (4), MACEDON, THESSALY (3), PHOCIS, Thermopylae, Delphi, Delphi, BOEOTIA, Thebes, Asopus, Plataea, Cithaeron, EUBOEA, Marathon, Athens, ATTICA (7), Eleusis, Megara, Salamis, Aegina, (2), (6), Corinth, Isthmus, Argos, PELOPONNESE, MESSENIA, Orestheiion, Sparta, LACONIA (8), N

Numbered key (bottom left):

1. Immediately after the battle of Salamis the Persian fleet sails east: some of it winters in Cyme and on Samos and the rest disperses.
2. The Greek fleet follows as far as Andros and disperses after operations there and in the surrounding islands.
3. Early October: the Persian army withdraws from Attica to Thessaly; Mardonius winters there and Xerxes returns home, escorted as far as the Hellespont by Artabazus.
4. After three months operations in Chalcidice, Artabazus rejoins Mardonius.
5. Spring: the Persian fleet regroups at Samos.
6. The Greek fleet assembles at Aegina and sails as far as Delos.
7. June: Mardonius overruns Attica and the Athenians evacuate to Salamis.
8. July: the Spartans march.

Scale: 100 miles / 100km

Persian treasure was a powerful lever of imperial power. Achaemenid gold armlets from the 5th century BC. British Museum.

beside him, and said, "This is Mardonius: he will pay the Spartans the compensation they are owed"' (VIII.113–14). Xerxes then carried on to the Hellespont with his main escort provided by Artabazus with a large contingent of Persian or Median troops, and the balance of the army. Both Herodotus and Aeschylus describe this retreat march as a catastrophic rout, but the 45 days it took to get from Thessaly to the Hellespont suggests a fairly relaxed pace. Also, Herodotus contradicts the traditional account by mentioning how men who fell ill were left to be cared for in friendly or subject cities on the way. Xerxes and the small part of the army left with him crossed back into Asia by ship, the bridges of boats probably having been dismantled as a precaution against the rougher autumn weather, rather than destroyed to add to the Great King's woes. Artabazus and his men set off to rejoin Mardonius in winter quarters but were delayed by rebellion which had flared up in Chalcidice. This was ruthlessly suppressed at Olynthus but the Corinthian city of Potidaea held out in a three-month siege, which the Persians finally abandoned early in 479 BC; in the summer the Potidaeans were able to contribute 300 hoplites to the Greek army at Plataea.

The Greeks followed the Persian fleet as far as Andros, probably not intending to risk a full battle in open sea where the still more numerous and 'better sailing' enemy would be at an advantage, but to make sure of their departure from Greek mainland waters. Themistocles was still in command and he then led a brief campaign to collect reparations by threats or actual force from islands and cities that had medized; this was not achieved in the case of Andros. By October the fleet had dispersed to home ports and the Peloponnesian army had pulled back from the defensive line at the Isthmus. The spoils were shared out and dedications made to the gods, commemorative monuments and memorials to the dead were erected, and the most deserving contributors to the victory at Salamis were honoured, Themistocles above all by the Spartans. The Athenians returned to their city and the villages and countryside of Attica to repair their temples and homes and attend to their land.

The following spring, Mardonius sent Alexander, king of Macedon, to offer the Athenians freedom and security in their own land, repairs to their temples and new land in addition, if they sided with Persia. The Athenians made sure the Spartans learned of this approach and delayed responding to it publicly until they could do it in front of the ambassadors that were rapidly sent from Sparta. Herodotus gives a version of the message they sent back: 'So long as the sun holds his present course, we will never agree terms with Xerxes. We will come out and defend ourselves against him, trusting in our allies and the gods and heroes he has insulted by burning their shrines and statues'. The Spartans made a counter-offer to look after all Athenian non-combatants for the duration of the war. The Athenians thanked them for their generosity but urged them to send their army to join them to confront Mardonius in Boeotia. Mardonius had probably made similar approaches to

other Greek cities, but he recognized as clearly as the Spartans that Athens and, in particular, her seapower were key building blocks of the alliance. Without further delay he led his army south. When he reached Boeotia and Thebes, his hosts advised him to make it his base and use bribery 'to split Greece apart', but Mardonius went straight on to Athens. The Athenians, once again, had to abandon their city and Attica and take refuge with their ships at Salamis. Mardonius repeated his offer using a different messenger. The Athenian Council (*boule*) held firm and one member, who had possibly taken Persian gold in return for proposing acceptance, was stoned to death, and his family afterwards.

The Athenians then sent a delegation to Sparta. They pointedly reminded the Ephors (the five-strong panel of chief-executive officials who governed alongside the twin kings of Sparta) of the Persians' offer, expressing their disappointment that the Spartans had not yet come to support them in the defence of Attica. They pointed out that, while it was too late to meet the Persians in Boeotia, they could still confront them in Attica on the Thriasian Plain, east of Eleusis. But they declared that, if the Spartans did not come north, 'the Athenians would find some way of looking after themselves without their assistance'. This not very veiled threat would have been a sharp reminder of Themistocles' warning in the previous year, that he would abandon Greece and lead a mass migration to the south of Italy, if the Peloponnesians abandoned Salamis to defend the Isthmus line (VIII.62). As at the time of Marathon, and immediately before Thermopylae, the Spartans were piously occupied with an important religious festival, on this occasion the Hyacinthia. However, at the same time and, perhaps not coincidentally, battlements were being added to strengthen the wall that had been built across the Isthmus in 480 BC; this work presumably employed Spartan manpower in spite of the festival. Then again, Herodotus and his sources may, for the sake of another tale of Spartan bloody-mindedness, have overlooked the fact that preparations were being made at the same time for a campaign of unprecedented scale and importance. Finally, the Spartans marched, leaving under cover of darkness without informing the Athenian delegation. Next morning, in a dramatic and bitter speech, the Athenians took the alliance right to the brink. They denounced the Spartans for 'keeping

View to the south-east from the area north of the river Asopus where the Persians built their fort towards the base of the Cithaeron Range and the position initially occupied by the Greek right and much of their centre. The line of small trees across the field in the foreground marks the remnants of the Asopus River.

45

Attica and Boeotia

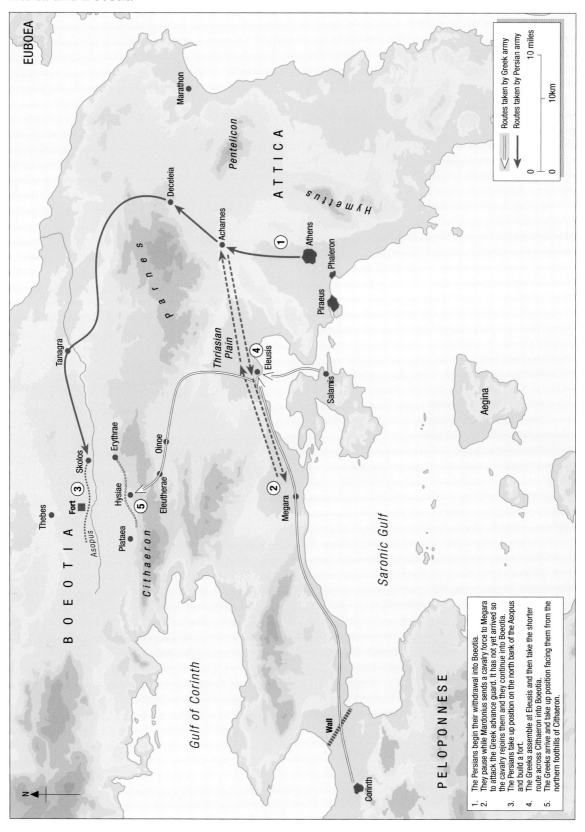

EUBOEA

Marathon

Pentelicon

A T T I C A

Hymettus

Deceleia

Acharnes

① Athens

Phaleron

Piraeus

P a r n e s

Tanagra

Thriasian Plain

④ Eleusis

Salamis

Aegina

Erythrae

Olnoe

Skolos

Fort ③

⑤ Hysiae

Eleutherae

Plataea

② Megara

Saronic Gulf

Thebes

B O E O T I A

Asopus

C i t h a e r o n

Gulf of Corinth

P E L O P O N N E S E

Wall

Corinth

N

Routes taken by Greek army
Routes taken by Persian army

0   10 miles
0   10km

1. The Persians begin their withdrawal into Boeotia.
2. They pause while Mardonius sends a cavalry force to Megara to attack the Greek advance guard. It has not yet arrived so the cavalry rejoins them and they continue into Boeotia.
3. The Persians take up position on the north bank of the Asopus and build a fort.
4. The Greeks assemble at Eleusis and then take the shorter route across Cithaeron into Boeotia.
5. The Greeks arrive and take up position facing them from the northern foothills of Cithaeron.

ABOVE
View a little west of south from the area of the Persian fort. The notch in the wooded ridge a little to the right of the lamp-post is where the pass over Cithaeron emerged into the foothills above the ancient village of Hysiae. The Greek left probably extended to some point in the area of modern Erythres, beyond the conifer plantation in the far middle distance. The Greek right occupied the forward slopes of the gentle 'Asopus Ridge' in the middle distance in the long middle phase of the battle.

BELOW
View north from the skirts of Cithaeron and the road down from the pass to the south-east of modern Erythres and looking over the area occupied by ancient Hysiae. Asopus Ridge is the central cultivated area beyond the line of trees; the Greek front may have run quite close to this line, in the area where the sharper slopes of Cithaeron level out. The Asopus River ran west to east north of Asopus Ridge and 3,000–4,000m (10,000–13,000ft) separated the two armies. A likely position for the Persian fort is to the left of the grey warehouse buildings towards the top right-hand corner of the picture.

the Hyacinthia and amusing yourselves whilst utterly betraying your allies' and continued, 'so, wronged by you and bereft of allies, the Athenians will make peace with Persia on whatever terms they can. That done, it is plain that we shall become the Great King's allies and march with him against any land to which the Persians lead us'. Whether or not, or whenever such a speech was actually made, it brutally spells out the mutual dependence of Athens and Sparta that was at the core of the defence of Greece, recalling the repeated hard negotiation that brought this critical alliance into being and held it together for just long enough. The Ephors coolly assured the Athenians that the army was now on the march to meet the 'foreigners' and had probably already got as far as Orestheion to the north-west of Sparta. This was not the shortest route to the Isthmus, but better for a large army and baggage train, and for picking up allies en route (VIII.140–44, IX.1–2).

In Athens, Mardonius soon heard that the 5,000 Spartans and the same number of Lacedaemonian *perioikoi* (citizens of communities in Laconia and Messenia that were closely affiliated to Sparta) were on the march with a very large number of support troops. So far he had spared the city and

Where it has not been developed in the modern era, the landscape at the base of Cithaeron may be very much the same as it was in the 5th century BC.

countryside from harm, hoping that the Athenians might agree terms, but now he ordered the destruction of everything that had been left standing in 480 BC or repaired over the winter. Leaving Athens blazing, Mardonius then began a withdrawal into Boeotia. Herodotus suggests three reasons for this move: that Attica lacked the open and level ground that was best for cavalry action; that he would risk being trapped in Attica if defeated, because there was only one, narrow route to the north (not actually the case); and that, fighting near Thebes, he would not only be in good cavalry country, but have a powerful, friendly city at his back. In fact, the Thriasian Plain was suitable, and there were several potential escape routes out of Attica. But Mardonius would have more room for manoeuvre in Boeotia and proximity to Thebes was probably the deciding factor. It was also advantageous to draw the Spartans further from home for psychological as well as logistical reasons, though there is no suggestion in the sources that this was part of the strategic thinking. Shortly after leaving Athens, Mardonius received a report that an advance guard of 1,000 hoplites had reached Megara and wheeled the army in that direction to deal with them, sending the cavalry ahead. They overran the countryside around Megara before being recalled by Mardonius when he learned that the Peloponnesians had got only as far as the Isthmus. However, this incident does suggest that he had not ruled out giving battle in Attica. He then resumed his withdrawal northwards via Decelea, entering Boeotia at Tanagra. The next day he took the army west along the river Asopus into Theban territory, lining it up on the north bank from a place called Skolos opposite Erythrae at the base of Cithaeron, to a point opposite Plataea. 'He cleared the land of trees, not out of hostility to the Thebans, but because he was in great need of a stockade to fortify his encampment to provide a place of refuge in the event that the battle did not go as he wished.... Each side of this fort was ten *stades*'. Clearing the land also made it better for cavalry and Herodotus uses the same verb, *keireein* (meaning 'shear, crop' and also 'shave'), when telling how the plain of Phaleron was prepared for successful cavalry action against a Spartan landing in 511 BC. The position of the fort is not known, but it was probably to the west of Skolos and just north of the Asopus covering the main road that ran north from the base of Cithaeron to Thebes. If laid out in the style of a Roman army camp, it has been calculated that this space of about 1,800 square metres (19,000 square feet) could have accommodated 70,000–80,000 men, including 10,000 cavalry. If Herodotus had the measurements right and it was intended that all the troops should fit inside, this is a challenge that he clearly ignores to his epic figure of (at least) 300,000 for Mardonius' army; but it doesn't necessarily mean that the army was as small as that and it would not have required much more than his round-figure space to accommodate 20,000 or so more (IX.13–15).

The Spartans and Lacedaemonians paused at the Isthmus and were joined by other Peloponnesians 'who chose the better cause'. They went on to Eleusis and joined up with the Athenians and other allies there. Later sources record that, around this time in 479 BC, an oath was sworn by all its members to sanctify and cement the Alliance. This is recorded in an inscription found in Attica and dated, problematically, to the latter part of the 4th century BC. It begins, 'I shall fight as long as I live, and I shall not value being alive more than being free' and goes on to pledge absolute loyalty to commanders and comrades, and perpetual friendship with 'any of the cities that joined in the fight'. If such an oath, the 'Oath of Plataea', was taken, this would have been the spirit of it and the gathering at Eleusis the most likely occasion; and, if there was such an oath, it proved to be effective. From there the whole army crossed Cithaeron to face the Persians. The allied fleet had reassembled in the spring at Aegina, but in much less force than for the previous year's naval campaign because it was necessary to retain sufficient manpower on land to oppose Mardonius' occupying army. In partial response to pleas from the Ionians to liberate them, the allies sailed east, but only as far as Delos. This was a good point in the middle of the Aegean from which to parry any new seaborne attack on the Greek mainland and, no doubt, selected for its significance as a Hellenic religious centre. Herodotus remarks that the Greeks were afraid to venture further outside their home waters, whilst the barbarians were too terrified to advance further west than Samos, 'so fear formed a barrier between them' (VIII.131). In fact, those waters were quite familiar to the Greeks but caution was justified if the Phoenicians were still with the barbarian fleet.

PLATAEA

Archer in 'Scythian' dress with hoplite. Note that the hoplite holds two spears, giving him the option to throw one before using the second for thrusting; this may have been the norm for most of the archaic era. The successful action against the Persian cavalry was spearheaded by an agile mixed force and concluded in a large-scale mêlée which was very different from the orthodox model of hoplite warfare. Early 5th century BC. Metropolitan Museum of Art, New York.

OPENING ACTION

The Greeks came over Cithaeron and manoeuvred east towards Erythrae and west beyond Hysiae to form a defensive line facing north and extending 6,000–7,000m (20,000–23,000ft) along the foothills. The rising ground gave them some frontal protection from cavalry attack, and each flank could have been protected by spurs, at the exit from the pass on the left and one of the more pronounced features on the right; they may also have relied on screens of *psiloi*. They favoured a static defence in as strong a position as they could find. The Spartans led the march through the pass and then east along the foothills to take their place on the right of the line. The Greek left deployed to the west with the Athenians on the flank. Mardonius made no move to prevent the Greeks emerging from the pass and forming up to face him. This option, if actually considered, may have been rejected because it would have meant fighting on ground that was not of his choosing and in circumstances that might prevent a decisive outcome by allowing a large part of the opposing force either to fall back on the pass or simply to remain in it, defending a narrow front in depth. This would have been a far more substantial impasse than encountered by the Persians at Thermopylae. It was now late July and this confrontation could actually have been forced months before after the re-invasion of central Greece and Attica. But there had been the not unreasonable expectation that diplomacy or subversion could divide the Greek alliance and bring about an easier victory.

The two armies, now about 5,000m (16,000ft) apart, may have faced each other for a few days, before Mardonius finally took the initiative and sent in his cavalry. His purpose was to soften the Greeks up and ideally break them, or to provoke them into coming down from the higher ground. The cavalry did find a weak point in the part of the line held by the Megarians but an elite squad of Athenian hoplites and the Athenian archer regiment

1. The Persian cavalry advance across the Asopus and form up on the Thebes–Hysiae road.

2. They harass the Greek line charging in waves from left to right and probing for weak spots.

3. The Megarians, positioned to the right of the Athenians, start to crumble but the Athenian archers are sent forward to attack the Persian flank.

The battlefield of Plataea

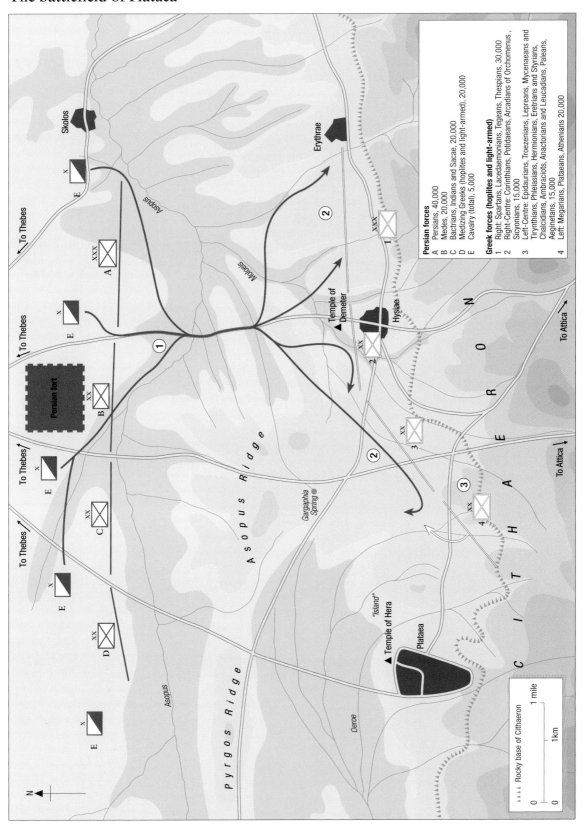

Persian forces
A   Persians, 40,000
B   Medes, 20,000
C   Bactrians, Indians and Sacae, 20,000
D   Medizing Greeks (hoplites and light-armed), 20,000
E   Cavalry (total), 5,000

Greek forces (hoplites and light-armed)
1   Right: Spartans, Lacedaemonians, Tegeans, Thespians, 30,000
2   Right-Centre: Corinthians, Potidaeans, Arcadians of Orchomenus ,
     Sicyonians, 15,000
3   Left-Centre: Epidaurians, Troezenians, Lepreans, Mycenaeans and
     Tirynthians, Phleiasians, Hermionians, Eretrians and Styrians,
     Chalcidians, Ambraciots, Anactorians and Leucadians, Paleans,
     Aeginetans, 15,000
4   Left: Megarians, Plataeans, Athenians 20,000

THE ATHENIAN ARCHERS HOLD THE LINE (pp. 52–53)

'As the Greeks were not advancing into the plain, Mardonius sent in all his cavalry. Their commander was Masistius, of great renown amongst the Persians, riding a Nisaean horse with a golden bit and magnificent trappings. His horsemen charged up to the Greek lines and attacked them in waves, harassing them painfully and calling them women.' (IX.61–62) The Megarians (1), 3,000 hoplites strong, were opposite a wide area of flatter ground on a spur of the foothills of Cithaeron. This enabled the Persians to concentrate their efforts here, charging in waves, wheeling and showering them with arrows and javelins as they passed across their front from left to right then falling back out of range of the modest response which was all the Greeks were capable of (2). Increasingly hard pressed, the Megarians sent a message to the Greek generals calling for urgent support and threatening to retreat. Herodotus writes that Pausanias called for volunteers to relieve the Megarians and that only the Athenians were willing to do this. They sent '300 picked men' (logades) with their unit of a few hundred archers. The 300 seem to have been an elite group of hoplites at their physical peak and more highly trained than the rest of the Athenian army. Other states, most notably Sparta with its 'knights' and Thebes with its 'sacred band', are known to have fielded similar units.

The Athenian archers and hoplites with their light-armed attendants took up a position out in front of the Greek line (3), having doubled out to flank the Persian cavalry in a lull between attacks. Their commander was Olympiodorus, son of Lampon (4). Masistius (5) continued to press the Greeks, leading the charge, but 'his horse was hit by an arrow in its side, reared up with the pain and threw him. The Athenians rushed him as he fell'. He died fighting, but he was not easy to kill. 'Under his purple tunic he wore golden scale armour, and their blows had no effect until someone realized what was happening and stabbed him in the eye.' Plutarch's account of the battle adds the detail that Masistius was wearing a closed helmet and that 'the butt-spike of a javelin was used' (Aristides XIV.5). The Persian cavalry did not notice they had lost their commander at first, but then they gathered together and charged in a mass rather than in waves to try to recover his body, and called for support from the infantry. The Athenians were now under great pressure, but support came up before the Persian infantry arrived and the cavalry were finally beaten back. The Greeks were left with a bloody trophy and greatly increased confidence. Masistius' body was paraded along the Greek line in a cart (suggesting their position was close to the tracks that connected the towns on the foothills of Cithaeron) and much admired. He was extravagantly mourned in the Persian camp.

was called up and killed their commander Masistius and the attack was beaten off after a fierce mêlée. Herodotus is suspected of playing to his Athenian audience by singling them out for their part in this incident and also by tainting the Megarians, enemies of Athens before and after Plataea, with the dishonourable intention of abandoning their position in the line. But only the Athenians brought a unit of archers to Plataea and they were conveniently positioned quite close to the Megarians if the Greeks were lined up broadly as detailed by Herodotus at the beginning of the second phase of the battle.

Encouraged by their success against the Persian cavalry, the Greeks decided to advance to the north-west to a position on the undulating ground immediately to the south of the Asopus, 'a better place for an encampment with a better supply of water'; the accessibility of a spring called Gargaphia, whose location can now only be guessed, was an important consideration. The Persians would certainly have observed this manoeuvre and it presented them with an opportunity to attack the Greeks whilst they were on the move with inevitable loss of cohesion. But Mardonius did not try to exploit this. He may have been content to allow the Greeks to move towards more open ground, which was where he wanted them, and to stretch and expose their supply line. In any case he needed to rest his cavalry, customarily the attack spearhead. Herodotus' topography is, as always, vague and his naming of two landmarks, a shrine dedicated to an obscure hero called Andocrates and the strategically important spring, is not helpful because their location is now unknown, though both appear to have been some distance back from the river. Nor does Herodotus give any chronological information up to this point, but after the fighting and the parading of Masistius' impressive corpse it is unlikely that this movement was carried out on the same day (IX.19–25).

Panel from the frieze on the temple of Athena Nike on the Acropolis, part of a sequence celebrating victory over the Persians in heroic style. To some this would undoubtedly recall the fight over Masistius' body. This temple replaced one on the same site, destroyed by the Persians in 480 BC. British Museum.

MIDDLE PHASE (10–11 DAYS)

At this point Herodotus sets out the Greek order of battle. He prefaces this with an account of a dispute between the Tegeans and the Athenians, each claiming the left flank, the second most honourable position in the line (no one disputed the Spartans' claim to the right). The Athenians won the argument by citing a number of legendary deeds from their past and pointing out that they alone of all the Greeks had stood against the barbarians and been victorious, temporarily forgetting the Plataeans who had fought beside them at Marathon. Herodotus does not mention another powerful consideration, that the Athenian hoplite contingent was over five times larger than the Tegean and, uniquely, further reinforced by archers. The Tegeans were, diplomatically, stationed alongside the Spartans, destined to play a critical part in the final phase of the battle. There probably was considerable debate along these lines, also involving other contingents. But it is likely that the battle order was settled before the army marched from Eleusis, and it is very unlikely to have been left

as late as Herodotus records, to be done in the face of the enemy. Following normal practice before battles, each commander had his seer carry out sacrifices and pronounce on the omens. The omens were the same for each side, victory in a defensive battle but defeat for either if they took the initiative and crossed the Asopus to attack. Both commanders were satisfied with this divine guidance, which most likely reinforced their own tactical assessments, and the two armies settled down and waited, taking no further action for a week or eight days. Each was in position on ground on which he believed he could fight most effectively. The Greeks were well placed for static defence, protected on much of their front by rising ground and by gullies or steeper inclines on each flank. The Persians were drawn up on the flatter ground north of the river, more suitable for cavalry action and the more expansive manoeuvring that their lighter infantry was capable of, and improved by extensive tree-felling. The river was only a modest obstacle, but the commanders on both sides would have been aware that a large force attempting to cross it in formation would inevitably lose cohesion. Mardonius, with Thebes and subdued central and northern Greece at his back and his logistics well organized, was more comfortably placed than Pausanias. His best troops were veterans of long

THE PERSIAN CAVALRY CUT OFF THE GREEK SUPPLY COLUMN (pp. 58–59)

After a week of inaction and perhaps occasional skirmishes, Mardonius sent cavalry under cover of darkness to the foot of the pass down from Cithaeron. 'The horsemen's mission was not unsuccessful. They caught a column of 500 transports [*hypozugia*, lit. 'things under yokes', probably meaning ox-carts or a mixture of carts and pack animals of various kinds] and their attendants with supplies for the Greek army from the Peloponnese as they emerged from the pass onto the Plataean plain. Seizing their prey, the Persians killed without mercy, sparing neither attendants nor beasts. When they had had enough of slaughtering, they rounded up the remnants and drove them down to Mardonius and the Persian camp.' (IX.39) Herodotus describes Mardonius' purpose as cutting off the steady flow of reinforcements that, according to a Theban adviser, has been 'streaming in'. However, it is probable that the largest contingents of the Greek army had mustered in full force at Eleusis or, at latest, by the time they crossed Cithaeron. Latecomers were not likely to make a significant difference. But this was a good time to begin strangling the Greek supply line, when the food that the army had brought with it must have started to run out. The savagery of the Persian attack, including the slaughter of animals that could more usefully have been taken alive, suggests both frustration at having been held back for so long and vengeance for the loss of Masistius and their defeat in the first day's action.

The attack is pictured taking place as the early-morning haze clears; Cithaeron is in the background. The supply train, which probably stretched out over 2,000–3,000m (7,000–10,000ft), is snaking out of the foothills onto the edge of the plain **(1)**. A Helot carrying wine jars (*amphorae*) **(2)** and a slave attendant **(3)** try to escape. Escort *psiloi* **(4)**, one with a sling, the other armed with javelins and a wicker *pelte* shield, put up a hopeless fight. The Persian cavalry are in their element, circling and driving into a loose and lightly protected formation, shooting arrows and using their spears as missiles or thrusting weapons.

campaigns far from home. He could still reasonably hope that internal frictions, aggravated by hunger and fear, might cause the Greek alliance to collapse. A bloodless victory was probably too much to expect, but some contingents might yet medize and others might run. Perhaps only a few cities would ultimately be prepared to fight, Sparta for sure, Athens conceivably not. Then he would have an opportunity to exploit his superior mobility and missile firepower against a retreating and fragmented enemy. Pausanias, on the other hand, was in country that had already been stripped bare by the Persians and there must have been very little left in the way of resources to draw on in Attica. Greek armies normally carried just a few days' supply of food with them on campaign and otherwise expected to live off the land, by plunder or in more civilized fashion if they were in friendly territory. They had little experience of long campaigns. This was the largest Greek army ever to take the field and it was increasingly dependent as the days went by on a long supply line, a situation completely outside Pausanias' or any of his fellow generals' experience.

This extended stand-off could be evidence that neither commander felt he had sufficient numbers to be confident of success in an all-out attack. However, after a week, Mardonius sent cavalry under cover of darkness to the foot of the pass down from Cithaeron. There they cut off a large supply column and rounded up all the animals that survived the attack and drove them down to the Persian lines. In fact, Mardonius could have sent troops round either flank and to the rear of the Greeks at any time in the preceding week. Incompetence or lack of spirit cannot be ruled out, but it is hard to pin either on Mardonius. A prolonged stand-off was consistent with a waiting strategy. When the time came to fight again, he would have the Greeks in this more exposed position, weakened by days of uncertainty and dwindling supplies, and possibly attacking out of desperation or retreating in disorder. And the rewards for medizing, no doubt, remained on offer.

Slave, Helot or lower-class citizen carrying water or wine. The Greek defensive line could have been supplied with water from the springs and rivers by this method.

The remains of ancient Plataea seen from the north slope of Cithaeron. The Greek plan was to fall back overnight to the rising ground in front of the city and to its east.

Mardonius did not immediately follow up on his successful thrust behind the Greek lines: 'after this action they waited two more days, neither side willing to begin the battle. For although the barbarians kept advancing to the Asopus' edge to put the Greeks to the test, neither army actually crossed it' (IX.40). Here, Herodotus may be describing harassment that actually began on the first day of the stand-off at the river. In any case, the attack on the supply column, cutting off any subsequent replenishment, sharply increased the pressure on the Greeks. Herodotus increases the drama of his narrative with a four-part interlude. (It is worth remembering here Herodotus' earlier gentle disclaimer that, while he feels it is his duty to record everything he is told, belief is another matter in some instances, which he generally signals.) First, Artabazus, who was probably second-in-command, advises withdrawal within the walls of Thebes, where supplies are still plentiful, and to make lavish use of Persian treasure to buy Greek surrender. Mardonius overrules this (the army could not have fitted into the city and he must now have accepted that all efforts at bribery of the hard core of Greek resistance had failed) and gives orders to prepare to attack at dawn the next day, defying the still unfavourable omens. Then, in the middle of the night,

1. Day 1: the Greeks advance to a line along the river Asopus.

2. The Persians adjust their position to face them from the north bank the river. The two sides hold these positions for a week with little or no skirmishing across the river.

3. Day 8 (overnight): Mardonius finally acts and sends contingents of his barbarian cavalry round the Greek right to cut off the Greek supply train. Increased harassment over the next day or two keeps the Greeks back from the Asopus, out of bowshot.

4. Day 10 or 11: Mardonius' cavalry presses the Greeks from all sides and overruns and fouls the Gargaphia Spring, now a vital water source for the Greeks with access to the Asopus denied. The Greeks fall back onto higher ground where they can. Later the decision is taken to fall back closer to the base of Cithaeron during the night to take up a stronger defensive position with access to ample water.

The middle phase of the battle

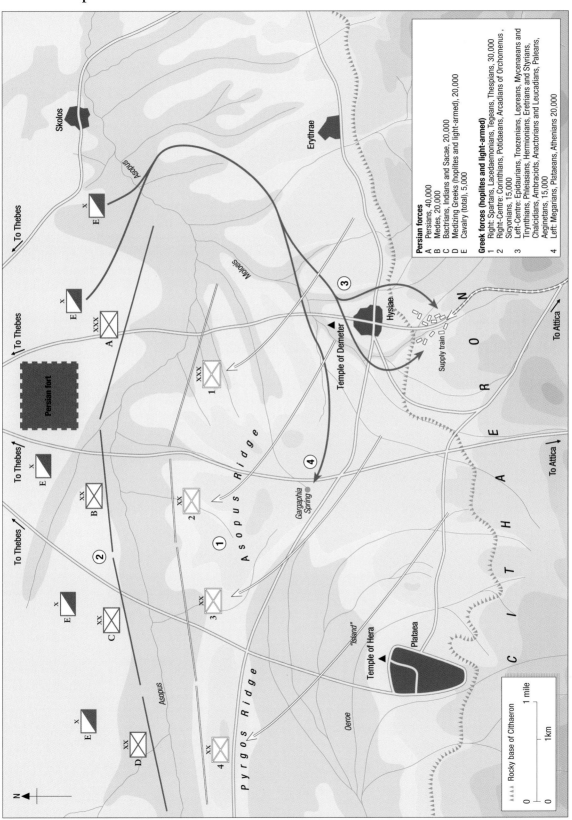

Persian forces
A   Persians, 40,000
B   Medes, 20,000
C   Bactrians, Indians and Sacae, 20,000
D   Medizing Greeks (hoplites and light-armed), 20,000
E   Cavalry (total), 5,000

Greek forces (hoplites and light-armed)
1   Right: Spartans, Lacedaemonians, Tegeans, Thespians, 30,000
2   Right-Centre: Corinthians, Potidaeans, Arcadians of Orchomenus , Sicyonians, 15,000
3   Left-Centre: Epidaurians, Troezenians, Lepreans, Mycenaeans and Tirynthians, Phleiasians, Hermionians, Eretrians and Styrians, Chalcidians, Ambraciots, Anactorians and Leucadians, Paleans, Aeginetans, 15,000
4   Left: Megarians, Plataeans, Athenians 20,000

Alexander of Macedon rides over to the Greek lines and warns the Athenian generals that the Persians are about to attack but advises them to wait patiently if this does not happen because the barbarians' supplies are running out and they will have to fight soon. Then at first light, to prepare for the anticipated attack, the Athenians and Spartans swap positions, so that the Athenians can face the Persians, because they 'fought with them at Marathon and understand their way of fighting' (IX.46). But the Persians also switch flanks and so Pausanias reverses the manoeuvre. Mardonius follows suit and they all end up where they started, tens of thousands of troops having covered several thousand metres in a round trip from flank to flank. This would have been a suicidal manoeuvre for the Greeks to undertake and Mardonius could not have failed to exploit it. This story has to be dismissed for its absurdity and as a clumsy, and unnecessary, counter to perceptions that the Athenians' involvement in the climax of the battle was inferior. Finally, Mardonius sends a herald to taunt the Spartans for their apparent reluctance to face his best troops and to challenge them to combat between equal numbers of picked men (for which there was a precedent in the mid-6th-century 'Battle of the Champions' between Sparta and Argos). The Spartans do not respond. Herodotus' sources may, in fact, have had some knowledge of formal or informal contacts between the two sides in the long days before the final battle as the Persians continued to probe for weaknesses in Greek solidarity.

Later in the day, according to Herodotus, Mardonius renewed and increased the pressure on the Greeks by attacking with his cavalry in full force.

View to the east from above Plataea. The town in the middle distance is Erythres. Ancient Hysiae was somewhere not far beyond its eastern edge. The Greeks' initial position curled below the bastions of Cithaeron to cover Hysiae and the exits to the passes into Attica. The area called the Island was somewhere between Plataea and Hysiae in the middle distance and the Greek plan, that was at best only partially executed, was to drop back from the Asopus and form a more defensible line from in front of Plataea to the east of Hysiae.

His horsemen rode up and mauled the whole Greek army with their javelins and arrows, and, as they were mounted archers, it was impossible for the Greeks to engage with them. They also fouled the spring of Gargaphia and blocked it up, and this was where the Greek army had been getting its water. The Spartans were placed closest to this spring but it was further away from the rest of the Greeks in their various positions, whilst the Asopus was within easy reach. But they had to go to the spring because they were kept away from the river and prevented from drawing water from it by the cavalry and their arrows. With the army now cut off from its water supply and severely harassed by the cavalry, the Greek commanders gathered together with Pausanias on the right flank to discuss these and other problems, because they had an even greater worry. They were out of food and the support troops (*opeones*) sent to the Peloponnese to fetch supplies were cut off by the cavalry and could not rejoin the army.

IX.49–50

Greece was closer to the 'razor's edge' than at any other moment in the war; Mardonius was winning the deciding battle. An earlier incident described by Herodotus gives an idea of the defensive tactics used by the Greeks, who were very probably under attack from behind as well as in the flanks and front. A force of 1,000 Phocian hoplites, 'certainly medizing, but against their will and under compulsion', arrived to join the Persian army at Thebes. Mardonius had them form up out on the plain and ordered his cavalry to surround them; Herodotus cannot say whether he wanted to test their mettle or had more vicious intentions. 'When the cavalry charged towards them as if to wipe them out and raised their javelins to throw (perhaps one of them even did), the Phocians faced up to them, drawing their ranks together all round and making the files as deep as possible. Then the cavalry wheeled and galloped away.' Mardonius commended the Phocians for their courage and urged them to fight well for Persia, probably quietly grateful for this tactical demonstration (IX.17–18). Thucydides usefully describes a battle fought in 423 BC between a force under the command of Brasidas, the great Spartan general, and a larger body of non-hoplite barbarian troops, in this case Illyrians. 'Seeing that the Illyrians were about to attack, he formed his hoplites into a square and placed his contingent of light-armed inside it and prepared to retreat. He positioned the youngest soldiers where they could dash out to meet an attack from any direction and himself stood ready at the rear with 300 picked men to make a stand against the leading ranks of the enemy to screen the withdrawal' (IV.125). The tactics here are more proactive and the mention of hoplite skirmishers (*ekdromoi*), of light-armed (*psiloi*) deployed amongst hoplites, and of the special role for the elite 300 (*logades*), suggests a degree of flexibility that many later descriptions of the classic phalanx would not seem to allow. It is possible to visualize the entire Greek army in a formation similar to Brasidas', or divided by main division into a number of squares or rough ellipses with light-armed sheltering inside, though skirmishers on foot would have been fairly ineffectual against mounted attackers. The Spartan's failure to defend the spring is intriguing, as is Herodotus' failure to criticize them for this, whether justified or not. However, the water would have been collected and carried by support troops rather than hoplites, maybe under cover of darkness and with a light-armed escort, if any. So the Persians may only just have discovered the spring's existence and its importance to the Greeks, and then moved too quickly for

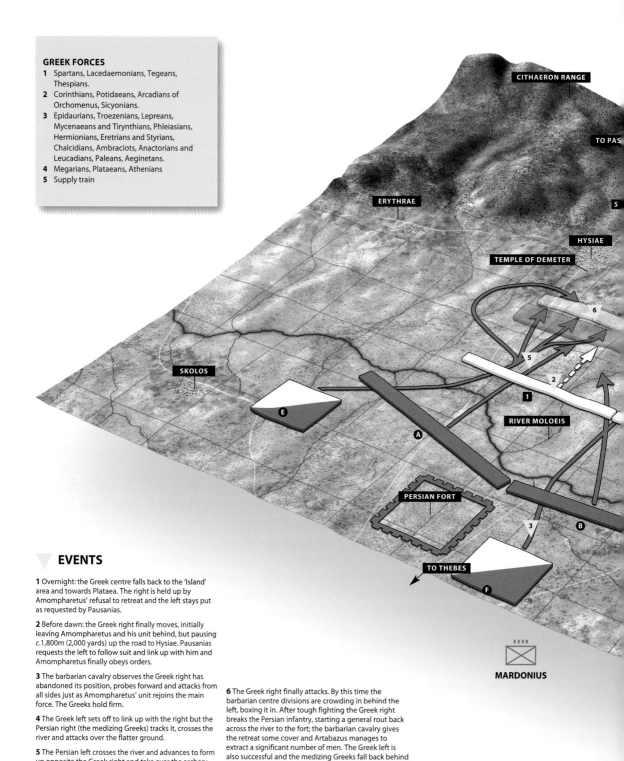

GREEK FORCES
1. Spartans, Lacedaemonians, Tegeans, Thespians.
2. Corinthians, Potidaeans, Arcadians of Orchomenus, Sicyonians.
3. Epidaurians, Troezenians, Lepreans, Mycenaeans and Tirynthians, Phleiasians, Hermionians, Eretrians and Styrians, Chalcidians, Ambraciots, Anactorians and Leucadians, Paleans, Aeginetans.
4. Megarians, Plataeans, Athenians
5. Supply train

CITHAERON RANGE

TO PAS

ERYTHRAE

5

HYSIAE

TEMPLE OF DEMETER

6

SKOLOS

5

2

1

E

RIVER MOLOEIS

A

PERSIAN FORT

3

B

TO THEBES

F

XXXX

MARDONIUS

▼ **EVENTS**

1 Overnight: the Greek centre falls back to the 'Island' area and towards Plataea. The right is held up by Amompharetus' refusal to retreat and the left stays put as requested by Pausanias.

2 Before dawn: the Greek right finally moves, initially leaving Amompharetus and his unit behind, but pausing c.1,800m (2,000 yards) up the road to Hysiae. Pausanias requests the left to follow suit and link up with him and Amompharetus finally obeys orders.

3 The barbarian cavalry observes the Greek right has abandoned its position, probes forward and attacks from all sides just as Amompharetus' unit rejoins the main force. The Greeks hold firm.

4 The Greek left sets off to link up with the right but the Persian right (the medizing Greeks) tracks it, crosses the river and attacks over the flatter ground.

5 The Persian left crosses the river and advances to form up opposite the Greek right and take over the archery bombardment from the cavalry. The cavalry withdraws to replenish missiles and to wait for the infantry to break the enemy line. The Greek right waits under the protection of its shields.

6 The Greek right finally attacks. By this time the barbarian centre divisions are crowding in behind the left, boxing it in. After tough fighting the Greek right breaks the Persian infantry, starting a general rout back across the river to the fort; the barbarian cavalry gives the retreat some cover and Artabazus manages to extract a significant number of men. The Greek left is also successful and the medizing Greeks fall back behind the walls of Thebes.

7 The Greek centre sets off to join the pursuit and rout but is outflanked by the medizing Greek cavalry and sustains quite heavy losses.

PLATAEA 479 BC

The final 24 hours of the battle sees the Greeks retreat before launching an attack which breaks the Persian line, leading to a decisive victory.

Note: Gridlines are shown at intervals of 1km/0.6 miles

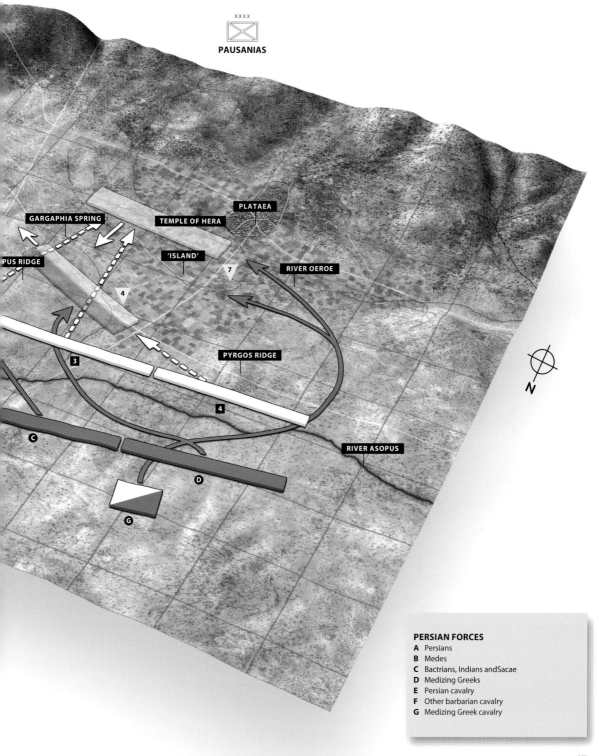

xxxx
PAUSANIAS

GARGAPHIA SPRING

TEMPLE OF HERA

PLATAEA

PUS RIDGE

'ISLAND'

RIVER OEROE

7

4

PYRGOS RIDGE

3

4

C

RIVER ASOPUS

D

G

N

PERSIAN FORCES
A Persians
B Medes
C Bactrians, Indians andSacae
D Medizing Greeks
E Persian cavalry
F Other barbarian cavalry
G Medizing Greek cavalry

any defence to be mounted. But, as Herodotus reveals, the Greek command had a bigger problem. They had run out of food and could not be resupplied because the Persian cavalry had cut them off from the supplies accumulating at the foot of the pass over Cithaeron. Also, several days' dense occupation of the same area of land by tens of thousands of men within a tight perimeter must have made the conditions increasingly foul!

FINAL PHASE: THE LAST 24 HOURS AND 'THE MOST GLORIOUS VICTORY EVER KNOWN'

> The outcome of the generals' discussion was a decision to fall back on 'the Island', if the Persians held off making an all-out attack for the rest of the day. This place is ten *stades* [1,800m] from the Asopus and the same distance from the spring of Gargaphia and the area where the army was now positioned, and is in front of the city of Plataea. It is a kind of landlocked island formed by the division of the river into two channels as it flows down from Cithaeron into the plain; the distance between the channels is about three stades before they join again. The river is called Oeroe, the daughter of Asopus according to the locals. The plan was to move to this place so that they would have a plentiful supply of water and protection from close-range attack by the cavalry. They decided to do this during the second watch of the night to prevent the Persians seeing them setting off and pursuing them with their cavalry and disrupting the move. Having reached the place... they intended to send half the army up to Cithaeron while it was still night to fetch the support troops who had gone for supplies and were cut off on the mountain. After this plan had been agreed the Greeks were kept under remorseless pressure by the cavalry for the whole day, but, when it was over, the attacks came to an end.

Evidently, Mardonius was not confident that he had sufficient numbers to succeed against a static hoplite defence, at least until his strategy of attrition had taken greater effect. But, though he did not yet know it, the Greeks were at last going to move, and the cohesion that they had so resolutely maintained was shortly to fracture.

> At the time of night that had been agreed upon for making their move, a large number of the Greeks set off, but they did not intend to take up the new position that had been agreed upon. Once they had got moving they were happy to keep on running from the Persian cavalry and carried on in their flight as far as the city of Plataea, coming to a halt at the sanctuary of Hera. This is just outside the city and 20 *stades* (3,600m) from the spring of Gargaphia.
> IX.51–52

The Island cannot now be identified, but the one dimension Herodotus gives suggests that the space would have been very crowded with tens of thousands of men on it and, even if the rivers gave them better protection than the features they had previously occupied, collecting water would be highly dangerous with archers lining the opposite banks. It is also hard to see the sense of assembling the whole army in this place and then sending half of it off to link up with the stranded supply train. It has been suggested that the whole manoeuvre was a ruse to entrap Mardonius somehow, as Themistocles lured the Persian fleet into the straits of Salamis, but there is no evidence to support such a theory, and

Hoplite and Persian engaging hand to hand as thousands did at the climax of the battle. The Persian's 'bonnet', *spara* shield, quilted tunic (which may have had small metal plates sewn into it) and exotic trousers are clearly depicted. The Greek is wearing a helmet with movable cheek-pieces, a type known as 'Chalcidian', an evolution which remedied the drawbacks of the more enclosed Corinthian helmet. He would surely have pulled them down shortly before charging, but the artist preferred to show his staunch profile to match his equally determined opponent's. The 'Brygos painter' treats the barbarian with the same respect as Herodotus does in his narrative. This painter was active during the first 30 years of the 5th century BC so this image has also been associated with Marathon. Ashmolean Museum, Oxford. (Nick Sekunda)

Herodotus would surely have told us if he had come across the slightest hint of it in his investigations! Equally, this does not seem to have been the start of a retreat to the Isthmus, which would have caused an immediate break-up of the Greek alliance. It was to be a forced regrouping, entirely defensive in purpose, and then the waiting was to continue amid the hope that the Persians might themselves run out of food or commit themselves in some way that would finally allow the Greeks to fight back in favourable circumstances.

The Greek contingents that retreated first and fell back further than ordered are not named by Herodotus, but his account of the final 24 hours of fighting strongly suggests that they comprised the entire central division, a hoplite strength of around 15,000, approaching half of the entire force. Whilst his language is not as vicious as implied by Plutarch's remark that 'he simultaneously accused them of disobedience, desertion and treachery' (*Concerning the Malice of Herodotus*, 42), Herodotus clearly sees them as 'running away', but does not dwell on the incident to the extent that he does in the case of the surrender of the Thebans at Thermopylae (VII.233) or the alleged flight of the Corinthians at Salamis (VII.94). In mitigation, these contingents had probably been under the greatest pressure from the escalating barbarian harassment, positioned as they were on lower ground between the ridges occupied by the right and left flank divisions. Secondly, they did not carry on over Cithaeron but halted on the plateau in front of the ruins of Plataea, a stronger defensive position because it was further up into the foothills and, of course, offered a shorter escape route to the passes. It could also have been that orders had not been clearly communicated to them or fully understood, or that they overshot their objective in the dark. An attractive alternative interpretation has Herodotus' sources, through ignorance or bias, misrepresenting a more straightforward plan for the whole line to fall directly back to a position closer to the base of Cithaeron stretching from in front of Plataea, across the Island and as far as the entrance to the pass above Hysiae, overlapping and to the west of the position they had first occupied.

'THE MOST GLORIOUS VICTORY EVER KNOWN' (pp. 70–71)

With the omens at last favourable, and the 1,500 Tegeans to their left already committed, the 10,000 Lacedaemonian hoplites and their light-armed support could at last go onto the offensive.

The Persians put away their bows and faced up to them. At first the fighting was along the wall of shields but, when this had been knocked over, there was a hard struggle around the temple of Demeter. It went on for such a long time that, for the Greeks, it came down to *othismos* [shoving with shields with the front lines locked together] because the barbarians kept grabbing their spears and breaking them **(1)**. The Persians were not inferior in courage or strength, but they were not armed like hoplites or trained in their way of fighting, and they did not have the tactical skill of their opponents. They were darting forward in ones and tens, gathering together in larger or smaller groups, hurling themselves at the Spartans and being wiped out. But wherever Mardonius **(2)** was fighting, mounted on his charger and surrounded by his thousand picked men, the best of the Persians, there they pressed the enemy hardest. While Mardonius lived, the Persians held out and struck down many Lacedaemonians as they defended themselves. But when Mardonius was killed and the best of the army who fought alongside him had fallen, then the rest were put to flight and gave way before the Lacedaemonians. Their greatest disadvantage was the lack of armour in their equipment. They were, in effect, light-armed (*gymnetes*, literally 'naked') battling with hoplites
IX.61–63

Herodotus notes with admiration that the barbarians put up a strong and courageous resistance, in spite of the disadvantages which he so clearly highlights. *Othismos* was an exclusive element of hoplite warfare marking the climax of conventional hoplite battles and the Greek need to adopt this tactic finally to break the Persians is testimony to their toughness as opponents, outgunned as they were. Herodotus' respect for Mardonius is equally clear, leading from the front as all the best ancient commanders did and dying his hero's death. Plutarch adds the detail that a Spartan called Arimnestos killed him with a rock, not a classic hoplite weapon. However, spears and swords broke in combat and then improvisation was an urgent necessity, as in the last stand at Thermopylae.

Pausanias **(3)**, his *linothorax* contrasting with his men's bronze cuirasses, has taken his place in the line as customary for Greek generals. There is apparently no evidence for the Spartans adopting the new form of body armour before it was abandoned altogether, but it would have been consistent with the character revealed by some of his behaviour after Plataea for Pausanias to arm himself more flamboyantly. Light-armed Helots **(4)** are intermingled with the hoplites, one throwing a rock, another bringing up replacement spears. A hoplite fights in the meantime with the butt end of his broken weapon **(5)** as the Greeks press against the remnants of the barbarian shield wall.

Pausanias saw [the Greek centre] moving off and gave orders to the Lacedaemonians to pick up their weapons and follow the others' lead, assuming they were on the way to the position that had been agreed. At this point all his commanders prepared to obey him, except for Amompharetus, son of Poliades, commander of the division (*lochos*) from Pitana [one of the five ancient villages which were combined to become Sparta]. He refused to run away from the barbarians and was unwilling to bring shame on Sparta. He was appalled by what was happening because he had not been included in the discussions that had taken place before. Pausanias and Euryanax were angered by this disobedience, but even more concerned that his refusal to move might cause them to leave the Pitana *lochos* behind. They were afraid that if they did what had been agreed with the rest of the Greeks and abandoned Amompharetus and his men, they would be deserting them to be wiped out. So, with this in mind, they kept the rest of the army where it was and tried to persuade Amompharetus that he was mistaken in what he was doing.
IX.53

Out on the left flank the Athenians were also staying put, suspicious, according to Herodotus, of the Spartan tendency 'to intend one thing but say something different', a reputation more justified by events that Herodotus had lived through half a century later.

When the Greek army began its move, the Athenians sent a horseman over to see whether the Spartans were setting off, or, if they clearly had no intention of changing position, to ask Pausanias what they were to do. The messenger arrived to find the Spartans in their original position and their leaders arguing.... As he argued, Amompharetus picked up a rock in both hands and threw it down at Pausanias' feet, saying that he was voting with this pebble [or *psephos*, used as a voting token in Athens but not in Sparta] against running away from the 'foreigners'. Pausanias told him he was raving, out of his mind. Then, when the Athenian delivered his message, he told him to go back and report on the situation and to request the Athenians to link up with the Spartans and do whatever they did in the withdrawal.
IX.53–55

Although Herodotus gives no sign of doubting any of this wonderful story, it is quite hard to take it at face value. However, looked at in the context of other information, it becomes more credible and illuminating in some respects. First, arguments of this kind, instances of disobedience and insubordination, even in the Spartan army, are documented elsewhere; strategy and tactics were collectively discussed and vigorously debated as often as handed down from the top. Secondly, there could have been challenges like this to the young and inexperienced Pausanias' authority. It is not actually clear where Amompharetus fitted into the Spartan order of battle; Thucydides in a brisk aside, possibly a professional jab at Herodotus, even says 'there was no such thing' as the Pitana *lochos* (I.20). However, it was probably a substantial unit of around 1,000 (representing a fifth of the Spartan contingent) with more numerous Helot light-armed troops, and the story may be an echo of its deployment as a 'rock-like' rearguard whilst the main body fell back towards the new line. In any case, things may not have been as chaotic as Herodotus' narrative suggests, but the situation was very serious. Certainly, the Athenians kept in close touch through the night with the movements, or otherwise, of all the contingents to their right.

Dawn came and 'the Spartans were still arguing, so Pausanias gave the order to move off, confident that Amompharetus would not allow himself to be left behind'. Amompharetus could not believe that Pausanias would abandon him until the rest of the Spartan contingent was well on its way. Then he finally led his men off 'at a slow pace' to rejoin the rest, who 'had gone about ten *stades* and then halted to wait for Amompharetus' unit.... Just as it reached them, the barbarian cavalry came up and attacked the whole force. They had followed their normal practice and, seeing empty ground where the Greeks had been drawn up on previous days, pushed forward and engaged as soon as they caught up with them.' It may have been a simple coincidence that Amompharetus rejoined the main force at exactly the moment when the cavalry caught up with it, but it is also possible to envisage a fighting retreat; if his *lochos* was approximately 1,000 strong with a larger number of Helots, he could have covered quite a broad front and, moving slowly, maintained a tight formation. The 'ten *stades*' (about 1,800m) covered by Pausanias before halting is a round figure which Herodotus uses often, in the way that the phrase 'about a mile' might be used. The movement was probably carried out by dividing into columns and re-forming into line on arrival, a drill of which the Spartans are known from later sources to have been masters. The new position was 'by the river Moloeis and in an area called Argiopium where a shrine of Eleusinian Demeter stands' (IX.57). The Moloeis has been identified as a stream running a little east of north down from Cithaeron into the Asopus. Unfortunately the location of Argiopium is unknown, but Plutarch places the shrine of Demeter quite near to the ancient village of Hysiae and there is some archaeological evidence to support this. Drawn up in close order and, for the sake of argument, eight ranks deep, his 11,500 hoplites (Spartans, Lacedaemonians and Tegeans) with substantial light-armed support would have formed an extremely solid front of at least

Typical landscape in the general area on the Asopus Ridge where Pausanias made his stand.

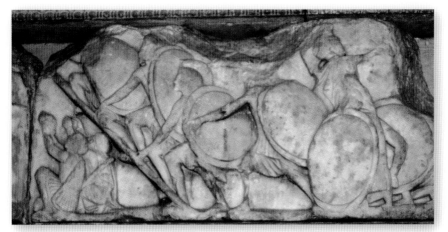

3,000m (10,000ft). The Moloeis and the gully it formed could have been sufficient to cover Pausanias' right and the terrain may have provided similar protection on the left, but it is possible the cavalry also got round his flanks and behind him. However, he was now closer to the main pass, an escape route if needed, and to the supplies that were stranded there and he had avoided the threat of being attacked on the move.

Mardonius, first given a moment by Herodotus to scoff at the cowardice of the Spartans and Artabazus' cautious advice to fall back on Thebes, led the Persian infantry at the double across the Asopus (ignoring his seers' repeated warnings that this would bring defeat). If his cavalry and the Greek right were out of sight, he would have known where they were from messages sent back and probably from the dust raised. Herodotus states that Mardonius thought he was pursuing the whole of the Greek army, but it is more likely that he was seizing what he saw as an opportunity to overwhelm one significant part of it by concentrating his cavalry and best Asian infantry. It was clear that the Greek centre had fallen well back and that their left had abandoned Pyrgos Ridge, though this division would have dropped out of sight behind the ridges and he may not have known exactly where it was going. 'When they saw the Persians charging off in pursuit of the Greeks, the rest of the barbarian contingents raised their standards and set off after them as fast as their feet would carry them. They were totally disorganized and not in any kind of formation, but streamed forward in a mass with a great deal of shouting; they were going to wipe the Greeks out' (IX.59). When the cavalry caught up with him, Pausanias had sent an urgent request to the Athenians to come to his aid in full force, 'or, if something has happened to make this impossible, we would be much obliged if you would send us your archers'. The Athenians were already on the way and making every effort to get over to support Pausanias, but the medizing Greeks on the Persian right had tracked their move to the east, crossed the river and attacked them. This was a battle on the same scale as Mantinea in 418 BC, the largest hoplite engagement of the Peloponnesian War and the largest fought between Greeks in the 5th century BC. Judging from Herodotus' disappointingly terse statement that 'the Boeotians fought the Athenians for a long time', the two sides must have been quite evenly matched; the Greeks totalled over 11,000 hoplites on Herodotus' count, assuming the Plataeans and Megarians were still with the Athenians, plus attendant *psiloi* and the Athenian archers. Herodotus adds that the medizing Thebans fought with great commitment, '300 of their foremost and best eventually falling at Athenian hands'. The Boeotian line finally broke and the survivors beat a rapid retreat to the protection of the walls of Thebes (IX.67). With both forces most likely moving in column as they converged, this would not have followed the pattern of an 'orthodox' hoplite battle and it is surprising that the Boeotian cavalry did not have any apparent impact in these circumstances. However they may have been elsewhere on the battlefield because Herodotus does mention their involvement later on. In any case, the Athenians had won a spectacular victory which was, unfortunately overshadowed by the even more spectacular victory that was being won a short distance away, a cause of resentment that coloured subsequent centuries' historical and biographical writing, particularly Plutarch's.

'So, the Lacedaemonians and the Tegeans stood alone'. The Persian cavalry harassed Pausanias' formation for an hour or more whilst Mardonius' infantry covered the 3,000–4,000m (10,000–13,000ft) from their position on the north side of the river facing the Asopus ridge. When the infantry arrived, the cavalry withdrew to rest their horses and replenish javelins and arrows, waiting for the moment to attack again when the Greek line broke. The massed infantry increased the pressure with a steadier and heavier barrage of arrows.

This late 5th-century painting of battle between gods and giants includes a good depiction of a Greek cavalryman in action against broken infantry. National Archaeological Museum, Athens.

The Greeks performed the sacrifices required before they could join battle with Mardonius and his army, but the omens would not come out right for them. During this time many fell and many more were wounded. The Persians had made a palisade from their wicker shields and were shooting arrows in a relentless shower. The Spartans were hard pressed and still the sacrifices were unfavourable. Then Pausanias turned his face towards the temple of Hera at Plataea and prayed to the goddess, begging her not let them be disappointed in their hopes. As he prayed, the Tegeans got to their feet, stepped out in front of the rest and advanced towards the barbarians. And, at that moment, just after Pausanias had said his prayer, the omens from the sacrifices at last became favourable, and the Lacedaemonians charged the Persians as well.
IX.61–63

The Greeks had endured the arrow bombardment, crouching, kneeling or sitting behind and under their shields, and taking casualties. Their body armour, helmets and shields were generally proof against the light Asian missiles but they could find their way through a helmet slit or a weak point in a *thorax*, or into an exposed neck, arm or leg. Herodotus describes one such casualty; Callicrates, 'who was wounded in the side by an arrow as he sat in his position while Pausanias was conducting the sacrifices' (IX.72). Light-armed troops amongst the hoplites huddled close and did what they could to protect themselves with their hide or wicker shields, if they had them. Sacrifice before battle was a highly important ritual and taken particularly seriously by the Spartans, and the signs from successive victims' entrails were unfavourable. The Tegeans may have been carrying out their own sacrifices with better results, or could no longer contain themselves. In any case, while Pausanias was still praying for divine assistance, 'they stepped out in front of the line and began to advance against the barbarians' (IX.62). By a happy coincidence the omens changed for Pausanias as the Tegeans moved off, and the delay in giving battle ultimately worked in the Greeks' favour by allowing time for the other barbarian contingents to crowd in behind the Persians, forcing them to fight the Greeks without the advantage of their greater mobility. If the Greeks charged at the double as at Marathon, Herodotus does not say so and the verb he uses (*chorein*) for both the Tegeans and the Lacedaemonians indicates a more measured advance. They were already in range of the Persian archers and it may have made better sense to stay at walking pace to keep in close order. Herodotus does imply that there was a period when there was enough space between the two lines to allow the Persians to skirmish forward and it may have been at this point in the battle that the Greeks named and honoured afterwards for their individual excellence particularly distinguished themselves by meeting them in front of the battleline.

Herodotus describes the barbarians' resistance and Mardonius' leadership with admiration and they fight on bravely even after the Greeks have pushed over their shield-wall and put them under the same pressure as they would have brought to bear on an opposing phalanx. But, finally, Mardonius is killed and the Persians break.

Aeschylus' almost contemporary account of the action on the island of Psyttaleia at the end of the battle of Salamis, describes an infantry action fought by a mixed force of hoplites and *psiloi* (though there were no archers in Pausanias' division):

> On the same day, fully armed in bronze,
> They leapt from their ships and made a circle
> All around the island. There was nothing our men could do,
> Nowhere to turn. Many were struck down by stones
> Flung at them, or by the arrows that showered from the bowstrings.
> Finally they charged in one great rush
> And hacked at the wretches' limbs and butchered them
> Until they had utterly wiped them out.
> *Persae 456–64*

Aristophanes' lines for his chorus of Athenian 'wasps', improbably well-preserved veterans of Marathon, treat the decisive advantage of the Greeks over the barbarians with dark humour: 'Then we chased after them, harpooning them through their pantaloons, And they ran for it, already stung around the jaws and eyebrows' (*Wasps* 1087–88). Persians, standing up to hoplites without the protection of a Corinthian helmet or a heavy shield, would have sustained terrible facial and upper-body wounds from overarm spear thrusts. The Greek word (*thunnazontes*) Aristophanes uses means 'spearing tuna', recalling Aeschylus' graphic description of the scene at the end of the battle of Salamis: 'The Greeks, like fishermen netting tuna or a haul of fish, Skewered and battered the barbarians with broken timbers and splintered oars And screams and groans filled the salty air' (*Persae* 425–27). Immediately after his account of the climax of the battle, Herodotus writes: 'And on that day, in accordance with the oracle, just compensation was fully paid by Mardonius to the Spartans for the killing of Leonidas, and the most glorious victory ever known was secured by Pausanias, son of Cleombrotus, son of Anaxandridas' (IX.64). Here he displays none of the caution with which he hedges his praise of the Athenian Themistocles as the architect of the previous year's successful defence. He rightly credits Pausanias and the Spartans with winning the war at Plataea and does not allow the conflicts and enmities of the decades that followed to cloud this statement.

Mardonius had indeed paid the price, but the battle was not yet over. The Persians retreated rapidly and the other barbarian contingents followed suit. Herodotus' language suggests that some of these had taken part in the fighting, but none had distinguished himself in any way. It was not an absolute rout, however. Herodotus records that the cavalry, including the Boeotians, became involved again and screened the retreating infantry, and that Artabazus succeeded in extracting a significant contingent, most likely Persians or Medes, though most likely a good many fewer than the 40,000 Herodotus allocates to him. He consistently presents Artabazus as the cautious veteran, disapproving of Mardonius' more aggressive strategies and, here, as keeping his men out of the battle and leading them off the field 'as soon as the fighting began, knowing full well what the outcome would be' (IX.66). However Herodotus also makes it clear that Artabazus' reputation did not suffer as a result of this disastrous defeat and he may actually have been credited for salvaging something from it. Additionally, 'the Persians and the mob of the rest of them' had time to get behind their 'wooden wall', man the ramparts and even strengthen them in some way, possibly with their wicker shields, before the Greeks arrived. News of victory on the Greek right reached the contingents of the central division that had retreated to Plataea in the night. Without forming into ranks they set off to join in the chase and elements were caught on level ground by the Boeotian cavalry covering the withdrawal. They suffered heavy casualties (600 dead out of the 4,000 Phleiasians and Megarians named by Herodotus) and were driven back to Cithaeron.

The Persians held out for a while in their camp and the Greeks made no progress until the Athenians arrived, 'because the Lacedaemonians had no understanding of siege warfare'. Herodotus credits the Athenians with finally scaling and breaching the wall but here he may be diplomatically offsetting his unqualified praise of the Spartans' victory. The Athenians seem to have acquired their experience in siege warfare later in the century, and, in any case, he then adds that the Tegeans were the first through the breach. Herodotus states that less than 3,000 barbarians survived the butchery that followed, and Persian losses would certainly have been very heavy, though not of the six-figure order of magnitude that his arithmetic implies. However his brief description of the final act rings true. 'When the wall went down, the barbarians could not form up in a solid mass. They had lost the will to fight, and, trapped in their thousands in a confined space, were out of their minds with terror. And the Greeks were ready to slaughter them' (IX.70). Total Greek casualties were undoubtedly much lighter but would have exceeded Herodotus' modest tally of 91 Spartans (including Amompharetus), 16 Tegeans and 52 Athenians. He earlier gives 600 as the number from the central division cut down by the Theban cavalry on the final day and makes reference to additional casualties in the opening clash at the base of Cithaeron, the successful Persian attack on the Greek supply train, and during the days of attrition in between. Subsequent deaths from wounds never seem to enter into the calculation, but the different Greek contingents left a large number of mass graves on the battlefield; a total body count in the low thousands is probably a reasonable estimate. Persian losses were probably between five and ten times greater (IX.70).

MYCALE

AMPHIBIOUS OPERATIONS

The Greek fleet was at Delos. Leotychidas, the Spartan king, was in command of the 110 triremes, less than a third of the force at Salamis. Herodotus does not detail the order of battle. However, as at Salamis, Athens probably supplied the largest element, maybe a third or more of the total and certainly a force large enough to besiege and eventually take Sestos at the end of the year's campaigning. Sparta would have supplied about ten ships, the same

Cape Mycale

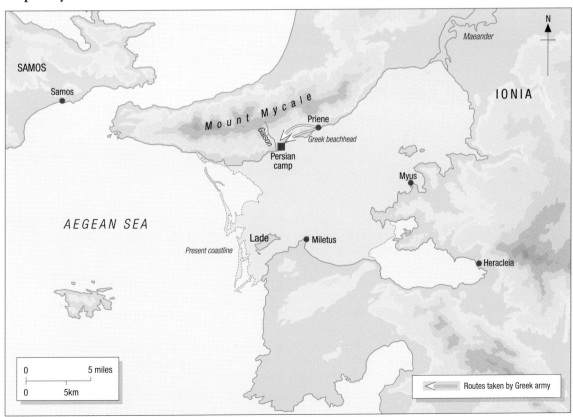

The 5th-century shore on
which the Greek fleet was
beached would have roughly
followed the edge of the
cultivated area.

number as at Artemisium, with Peloponnesian allies contributing a further
20–30. There would also have been quite significant contingents, ten or so,
from Aegina and Corinth. The Troezenians and Sicyonians, who respectively
sent five and 15 ships to Salamis, are listed, along with the Athenians and
Corinthians, as fighting with most distinction at Mycale. This force of a
maximum of 25,000 men was probably all that it was felt prudent to divert
from the land army that was to face Mardonius. Anticipating action on land,
it may have included over 3,000 hoplites, assuming an average of 30 per
trireme, the larger end of the scale of known fighting complements. On land
they could be supported by a significantly larger number of light-armed
troops drawn from the rowing and deck crews (which totalled around
22,000) and some of these may have doubled as hoplites. Thucydides briefly
describes a similar Athenian amphibious operation during the Peloponnesian
War: 'the rest of the army landed, that is, all of the crews except for the
thalamioi (oarsmen from the lowest tier, 54 per trireme) of over 70 ships with
whatever weapons they had with them' (IV.32). If each Greek ship also
carried a group of four archers, as was customary later in the century,
Leotychidas also had a useful counter to Persian firepower.

The Samians finally managed to persuade the Greeks that the Ionians were
ready to revolt as soon as support arrived. They told them that the barbarians
in Ionia could be easily overcome and that their ships were in poor condition
from having been at sea too long. So the Greeks sailed to Samos ready to
fight the Persian fleet there. However, the Persians were not prepared to face
them at sea. At this point or earlier, the Phoenicians, the best element of their
navy, had been sent home, presumably to protect Persian interests in the
eastern Mediterranean. The ships that were left were probably outnumbered
and, anyway, seem to have consisted of contingents from up and down the

The ridged terrain that slowed the advance of the Spartans and the rest of the Greek right.

eastern seaboard of the Aegean who could not now be relied upon, even if the crews were stiffened up, as in the previous year, with barbarian deck-fighters. They were beached where a stream called the Gaison flowed into the sea on the southern side of Cape Mycale. Their stockaded encampment had the protection of a land force commanded by Tigranes, the general of royal blood who had led the Median contingent in the previous year's invasion of Greece. After Salamis this contingent had stayed behind with Mardonius, but Xerxes had sent Tigranes to keep Ionia secure. Herodotus states he brought 60,000 men to Mycale but the actual number may well have been rather less than 10,000 Persians (perhaps a below-strength *hazabaram*). Assuming the fleet included the same complement of 30 barbarian troops per ship as in the previous year's campaign, its arrival would have added around 3,000 trustworthy infantry. Tigranes' force also included Ionian Greeks, but he took the precaution of disarming the Samians and positioning the Milesian contingent well away from the camp 'because these, of all the Ionians, were the ones they thought most likely to turn against them, given the opportunity'. This suspicion was reinforced by a Greek herald offshore calling out a message from Leotychidas, urging all Greeks on the Persian side to 'think of freedom before all else'. Significantly, Tigranes had no cavalry with him.

The 5th-century shore may have run along the line of greenery just beyond the telephone pole. The Greek left advanced across this level ground from the east with the southern slopes of the ridge on their right. The Persian camp can be envisaged below the hillock on the left of the picture.

THE GREEK LEFT STORMING THE PERSIAN CAMP AT MYCALE (pp. 82–83)

Leotychidas took his ships past the Persian camp and 3,000–4,000m (10,000–13,000ft) further into the bay and beached them, possibly just to the west of the city of Priene, and disembarked his men unopposed. They immediately formed up and advanced to the west in two divisions, left and right, about equal in size. The former, comprising the Athenians, Corinthians, Sicyonians and Troezenians took a direct route along the shore and the level ground beside it. The latter, comprising the Spartans and the rest, had to negotiate a ravine and hilly ground in a circuit that took them inland. The Persians formed up in front of their stockade and the left division attacked immediately whilst the Spartan division was still out of touch.

As long as their wicker shields remained standing, the Persians put up a good defence and held their own in the fighting. But when the Athenians and the rest of the division increased the pressure, urging each other on to finish the job and deny the Lacedaemonians any credit for it, then the situation changed. Breaking through the shield wall, they fell on the Persians, sweeping forward in a mass. The Persians absorbed the attack and held out for quite a while but finally beat a retreat to their stockade. The Athenians, Corinthians, Sicyonians and Troezenians [the order in which they were positioned in the line] hotly pursued them to the palisade and poured in behind them. With their palisade breached, the barbarians put up no

more resistance and tried their best to escape, all except the Persians. They fought on in small groups against the Greeks who continued to stream in.… Tigranes died fighting.
IX.102

The Spartans arrived in time to help with the mopping up and, at some point in the battle and taking a lead from the Samians, the Ionians in the camp turned on their barbarian masters whilst the Milesians posted outside did all they could to prevent any escaping. Herodotus ends his brief account of this battle with the words: 'And so Ionia [here meaning the entire community of Asiatic Greeks] broke away from Persia for the second time'.

The Persian fort is shown as quite elaborate (their camp on the north side of the Asopus was probably more substantial). It enclosed their beached triremes (1) as well as their infantry encampment. The Athenians are fighting their way through a breach created alongside the east gate and a seaman is using a grapnel to enlarge it (2). Some Persians have been caught on the wrong side of the gate (3). Ships' archers, and seamen and rowers fighting as *psiloi*, are mingled with the hoplites (4). Leotychidas' right division (5) approaches from the north and the lower slopes of the Mycale ridge.

Unfortunately, Herodotus gives only a little more space to the fighting (IX.102–4) than to various elements of the tradition that the victories at Plataea and Mycale were won on the same day, a coincidence that delights him, including the heartening rumour that Pausanias had won a great victory and the auspicious discovery of a herald's staff at the water's edge. The Greeks rowed past the Persian camp along the coast towards Priene and beached their ships along the shore to the west of the city. They disembarked and formed into two divisions. 'The Athenians and those contingents deployed with them, about half the Greek strength, advanced along the level ground of the beach, but the Spartans and those with them, had to cross a gully and ridges. While they were still making their way, the other division engaged the enemy.' The Persians held out behind their wall of wicker shields for some time and did not immediately break when the Greeks had pushed through it, but they were eventually pushed back into their camp. The Greeks fought their way in behind them and, at this point, the Spartan-led right division arrived to help finish the barbarians off. They burned the camp and ships and sailed back to Samos (IX.100–1). The neat parallels with the final day's action at Plataea and the balancing emphasis on the decisive contribution of the Athenians arouse suspicions of biased creativity on Herodotus' part. However, there are also important contrasts, for example, Tigranes' lack of cavalry, his well-founded distrust of the Ionian levies and resulting numerical weakness, and the reversal of the situation at the beginning of the last day at Plataea with the Greeks on the defensive and the Persians taking the initiative. Leotychidas' aggressive and high-tempo generalship was admirable. Tigranes had very limited options in the hopeless position in which he found himself. And the course of the fighting as described is consistent with what is known of other clashes between Greeks and barbarians, and with the nature of the opposing forces and the probable strength of each at Mycale.

Athena victorious, holding the stern-post (*aphlaston*) ripped as a trophy from a Persian ship. Attic, 480–470 BC, Metropolitan Museum of Art, New York.

AFTER THE BATTLES

A few days after honouring the men who had fought best at Plataea, burying their dead and sharing out the spoils, the Greeks laid waste the land around Thebes, whatever was left after Mardonius' occupation and battlefield preparation, and attacked the city. It held out for about three weeks until the Thebans agreed to give up the leaders of the dominant faction that had supported Persia. The army then dispersed. Immediately after the victory at Mycale, the Greeks returned to Samos and debated the future of the Ionians. The Spartans proposed evacuating them, bringing them west and resettling them in the trading centres (*emporia*) of Greek states that had medized. The Athenians strongly and successfully opposed this and the Ionians who had broken away from Persia again were sworn into the Hellenic Alliance for their long-term protection. The fleet then sailed to the Hellespont. According to Herodotus their mission was to destroy the bridges of boats, but he tells us earlier that they had been broken up in a storm by the time Xerxes reached them on his retreat after Salamis. In any case, Leotychidas found them gone and took the Peloponnesian contingent home. However, Xanthippus and the

Battle at the gates. The metal weapons have not survived but the hoplite in the attackers' front rank is clearly flanked by an archer with his bow drawn. Nereid Monument, British Museum.

Athenians decided to stay and 'make an attempt on the Chersonnese', which commanded the vital sea lane from the Black Sea. The area had previously been colonized by Athens until the Phoenicians had driven out Miltiades, the hero of Marathon, in 492 BC. The Athenians laid siege to Sestos, the strongest city on the peninsula, and, late in the autumn, eventually starved the defenders out. The Persian garrison made an unsuccessful attempt to escape and the city was taken. It quickly became one of Athens' most important overseas naval bases. The massive cables for the Persian bridges had been stored there, presumably for possible reuse and suggesting dismantling rather than destruction, and the Athenians took them home as trophies.

Herodotus' *Historia* ends at this point and this is where Thucydides begins his summary of the 50-year period in which the power of Athens grew and the Peloponnesian War became inevitable (I.89–118). Immediately after Plataea the Athenians returned to Attica and set about rebuilding their city and its walls. The Spartans and their allies, nervous of Athens' newly acquired strength, tried to persuade them to keep Athens unfortified. They argued that all Greek cities outside the Peloponnese should be left open to prevent the Persians from using them as bases as they had used Thebes, if they invaded again. For the Spartans, of course, it was a matter of pride and principle that their city was not walled. Themistocles, back in the centre of things, advised the Athenians to send the Spartan embassy home promising that an Athenian delegation would soon come after them to discuss the issue in Sparta. He then asked to be sent ahead with the rest of the delegates to follow only when the walls had reached a defensible height. Themistocles was able to play for time, trading on the personal friendship and respect he had built in the previous year, and then resorting to blatant disinformation. At his suggestion the Spartans sent a new delegation to check whether the rumours of intense building activity were true. This was, in effect, held hostage until the

Column drums from the wreckage of the unfinished temple of Athena, destroyed by the Persians in 480 BC, were built into the ramparts of the Acropolis in the hasty reconstruction work masterminded by Themistocles in the autumn of 479 BC.

Athenians were ready to send the rest of their delegation, which included Aristides. Themistocles was then able to announce formally that the city was fortified. He accompanied this with a lecture on the Athenians' right to self-determination, emphasizing their proven ability to identify what was in their own best interest and also in the best interest of Hellas, closing with the assertion that either all members of the Alliance should do without city walls, or they should all have them. However, 'the Spartans did not make any show of anger with the Athenians... but were privately annoyed at failing to achieve their purpose'. The Athenians went on to fortify the port of Piraeus in the following year under Themistocles' direction, completing the work he had set in train 15 years before and thus 'laying the foundations of empire'. Meanwhile, Pausanias took a fleet to Cyprus, conquered most of the island and then sailed north and took the city of Byzantium from the Persians, gaining control of the Bosporus. However, the rest of the Greeks rejected Spartan leadership on the grounds that Pausanias had begun 'to act more like a tyrant than a general' and placed themselves under the Athenians, who almost immediately started to collect contributions (*phoros*) from their allies to support the collective war effort under the terms of a new alliance. These funds were administered by Athens but held on the sacred island of Delos, and the voluntary confederation known as the Delian League came into being. It was successful in its purpose and, by the time of its great victory over the Persians on the Eurymedon River in 467/6 BC, controlled the whole of the eastern Aegean and the western coastal strip of Asia.

Xerxes was assassinated in 465 BC and was succeeded as Great King by his son, Artaxerxes. Five or six years later there was, yet again, a major revolt against Persian rule in Egypt and the Athenians sent a large fleet and army to support it. Artaxerxes tried without success to bribe the Spartans to invade Attica to make the Athenians leave Egypt, but he then subdued the revolt by direct force and eventually defeated the Athenians and their allies after a long siege on an island somewhere in the Nile delta. In 454 BC the treasury of the Delian League was moved to Athens and around this time its members began to be referred to as 'the cities that the Athenians rule' and were treated as such. By the end of the decade hostilities between Greece and Persia seem to have come to an end. There is uncertainty whether a formal treaty (the so-

This Athenian vase dates from 460–430 BC, the final decades of conflict between Greeks and Persians. It depicts combined-force action, hoplite and archer side by side, similar to that which opened the fighting at Plataea. British Museum.

called Peace of Callias) was actually agreed. However, increasing friction between Athens, and Sparta and her Peloponnesian allies had culminated in the first major clash between the two sides at Tanagra in Boeotia, and conflict much nearer home had become the overriding strategic priority. In the decades that followed, Persia interfered from time to time in Greek affairs on their western borders and Artaxerxes was still attempting to open negotiations with Sparta when he died in 424 BC. He was succeeded by Darius II, who took a closer interest in Ionia after the disastrous Athenian failure in Sicily in 413 BC. He succeeded in forming an alliance with Sparta the following year with the purpose of winning back the Empire's former subjects. Persia's support was not as consistent or wholehearted, nor the relationship as close as initially envisaged at the signing of this treaty, but it contributed significantly to Sparta's final victory over Athens in 404 BC. In 387 BC, in the reign of Artaxerxes II, the King's Peace guaranteed the autonomy of Greece that had 'hung on a razor's edge' in 480 and 479 BC. But the main condition was that the Greek cities of Asia, and the island of Cyprus be recognized as Persian possessions, more or less full circle from the Ionian Revolt, which had been 'the beginning of evil events for Hellenes and barbarians alike' (Herodotus V.97).

THE BATTLEFIELDS TODAY

PLATAEA

A car and at least a full day are necessary. G. B. Grundy spent a pioneering two weeks crossing and recrossing the site whilst W. Kendrick Pritchett seems to have made a life's work of it (Grundy, 1894; Pritchett, 1957 to 1985). Thebes (*Thiva*) makes a good base for an overnight stay, though sadly nearly all of its millennia of myth, legend and history are buried in layers under the modern town and its important museum has, at the time of writing, been closed for some years for reorganization and expansion. However, there are decent hotels and restaurants. The city is 90km (56 miles) from Athens and most easily reached by taking the E75, which roughly follows the route taken by Mardonius when he withdrew from Attica. A more interesting and rather slower alternative, calling for some wily navigation, is to go via Perama to get views of the island and straits of Salamis and across the Thriasian Plain and, from Eleusis (*Elefsina*), to follow the route taken by the Greek army over Cithaeron. There are excellent views of the whole battlefield from the road as it winds down from the pass and approaches modern Erythres, which is a little to the west of the likely site of ancient Hysiae. At Erythres it is easy to pick up the minor road that runs east along the base of Cithaeron and the line of Pausanias' opening position which extended from the exit of the pass 5–7km (3–4 miles) in the direction of Dafni. Rising ground to the west of Erythres could have covered the Athenian left flank and to the east there is a succession of spurs, one particularly pronounced, that could have anchored the Spartan right. Ancient Erythrae (after which modern Erythres is confusingly named) is generally accepted to have been a little to the west of Dafni. Grundy thought the landscape was little changed from the time of the battle and this was most likely true as far as the patches of cultivated vineyards, olive and fruit trees, and woodland were concerned. The various streams running down from Cithaeron were probably as numerous but unlikely to have all been following the same courses as in the 5th century BC. Certainly, in more recent decades, modern agriculture and the abstraction of water flowing down from Cithaeron for agricultural, domestic and industrial use have smoothed out what would have been a more varied and much more deeply etched landscape between the rocky base of Cithaeron and the river plain. However, the bones of the terrain must be broadly unchanged, not only at the base of Cithaeron but in the succession of low ridges that stretch down to and along the river Asopus. These may not appear to have much tactical

The names of 31 of the 44 Greek city-states recorded by Herodotus as fighting the Persians in 480 and 479 BC are inscribed on the Serpent Column. Minarets added to the 6th-century Christian basilica of Hagia Sophia in the 15th and 16th centuries can be seen to the right of the Obelisk of Theodosius, which was erected in the 4th century AD.

The Serpent Column was still intact in the late 16th century, as depicted in *Surname-i Vehbi*, a collection of Ottoman miniatures. Here, weavers process through the Hippodrome before the Sultan. Topkapi Museum.

significance to modern eyes but, in ancient warfare and for many centuries beyond, anything more than a gentle incline, rising even just a couple of metres, could give significant advantage to a defender.

The few visible remains of the city of Plataea are 4km (2 miles) to the west of Erythres. The battle gets its name because it was fought in Plataean territory; the city had been evacuated then burned down by the Persians in 480 BC and no fighting took place within or immediately outside its walls. A track leads up from behind the modern village (Kokla) to an abandoned hang-gliding centre on the 600m contour. From here there is an excellent view of the western half of the battlefield, diagonally across the ridges to its north-eastern corner and along the base of Cithaeron. Roads lead north-west and slightly east of north from Plataea to the opposite ends of the low but well-defined Pyrgos Ridge overlooking the Asopus, which was held on its forward slopes by the Greek left in the long central phase of the battle. *Pyrgos* means tower and there is a building (only a couple of centuries old), which is a useful landmark. Even now the ridge falls away quite steeply to the west and was as defensible against attacks from the rear as the front. Looking east from this ridge the ground falls away gently and then rises to the crest of the broad 'Asopus Ridge', which was held by the Greek right. It is also worth crossing the river and driving the short distance up to the village of Melissochori for a view of the Greek position from behind the Persian right. The Greek line may have extended as far east as the main north–south road between Hysiae and Thebes, but, in any case, its flank was probably protected by the gully carved by one of the tributaries of the Asopus flowing down from Cithaeron. The successful Persian attacks on the Greek supply train at the exit of the pass and on Gargaphia Spring somewhere behind the Spartan position, were probably launched from some distance to the east of this flank. The Asopus cannot really be described as a river now, at least in summer, but most of its course can still be picked out from a distance from the vegetation, shrubs and trees growing along. The only significant water feature on the plain is a stretch of the 190km (120-mile) Mornos Aqueduct that carries drinking water to Athens from the north-west, a more formidable tactical

The Parthenon, here showing the progress of the latest restoration work in May 2010, is one of the most powerful symbols of the flowering of Athenian culture. This could not have taken place if the war had been lost in 480–79 BC.

obstacle than the Asopus would have presented in the late summer of 479 BC. The Persians easily crossed it in force when they finally chose to and were able to drive the Greeks back from it as a source of water by shooting arrows at them from the north bank. The Greeks crossed it only during the final rout, so its exact location is not critical to the topography of the battle.

MYCALE

The battlefield can be conveniently included in a tour of the west coast of Turkey in a day that takes in nearby Priene, and perhaps Miletus or Ephesus, both also now landlocked. As at Thermopylae, the sea is now some distance from the battlefield, but the high cape must be little changed and it is easy to visualize the strip of shore and level ground that the Athenians advanced over, and the ridges that the Spartans had to negotiate. The site of the Persian camp and the precise location of the battlefield are unknown, but the village of Atburgaz is a likely spot. Samos is close to the tip of the cape.

Carry on north, stopping without fail at Pergamon and Troy, to Istanbul and stand in the Hippodrome of Constantine, or Sultanahmet Square, by the twisted bronze stump of the 7m (23ft) gilded 'Serpent Column' which was set up at Delphi to celebrate the Greek victory in 479 BC. Constantine the Great, Roman Emperor of the West and East, brought it here to this crossing point between Europe and Asia, East and West in the 4th century AD. Beyond, reliefs at the base of his column show Theodosius I, the late 4th-century Emperor of the East, in his pomp. The great basilica of Agia Sophia towers behind. These are massive symbols of the glories of Greece, the Roman Empire, Christianity and the Ottomans. The Sultanahmet 'Blue' Mosque is over to your right and Agia Sophia has four minarets, triumphs of Islam. 'Alternate history' is often just an entertaining game, but here the questions are really worth asking. If Plataea had been lost and Hellas had become part of a Persian Empire with southern Italy on its frontier, would Rome (that had turned republican at about the same time as Athens deposed Hippias) have grown to be the world power that Constantine ruled? If not, what of Christianity? If that religion had taken a different course, there may not have been the influences that shaped Islam. A Persian victory could well have changed far more than the scenery at the centre of the site of ancient Byzantium; it could have profoundly changed the cultural, intellectual, aesthetic, political and religious landscape of Europe.

FURTHER READING AND BIBLIOGRAPHY

It is a strange fact that, before 2010, there was not a single book in English, or any other language as far as I could see, on this enormous and very important battle, other than a slim but comprehensive survey of the literary sources published in 1904 (Wright) and an equally scholarly and detailed study of the battlefield's topography published in 1894 (Grundy). Of course, all accounts of the Persian War give reasonable space to Plataea and offer a fascinating range of often conflicting insights and interpretations. But, as Professor Jean-Nicolas Corvisier puts it, 'in the histories of the Persian War, this battle is often short-changed. It still deserves to be studied in its own right'. This is a (translated) quotation from his *La bataille de Platées, 479 av. J.-C*, a very welcome addition to the literature. His target audience is readers with a more general than military-historical interest in the ancient world so I hope my contribution will be a useful complement to his. Finally, I was fortunate to be able to read Professor Paul Cartledge's forthcoming book on the *Oath of Plataea* (2012) in manuscript, an intriguing exploration of a small facet of the Plataea story illuminating its broader historical and historiographical background.

The ancient texts, mostly Herodotus, are the critical source. Reflecting on the 'severe limits to our understanding', Professor Philip Sabin reminds us in *Lost Battles* that 'the ancient evidence that has survived is lamentably thin' and, comparing it to the mass of primary material on modern warfare that a writer can draw on, pictures 'an inverted pyramid in which modern scholarship teeters unsteadily above a narrow and unsatisfactory evidential base'. Narrow as it is, the base provided by Herodotus for a study of Plataea is by a long way the fullest surviving description of any 5th century battle, and later sources add very little specific information to this. The excellent 2002 Cambridge Greek and Latin Classics edition of Book IX (Flower) was particularly helpful; to quote its blurb slightly out of context, I found this commentary 'essential for exploring the meaning (or range of possible meanings)' of the text. Herodotus goes into little explicit detail on the tactics and methods of fighting used by the Greeks at Plataea because he could take his audiences' knowledge and understanding of what went on a 5th-century battlefield pretty much for granted. So it is not possible to build a narrative out of the quite fragmentary information he does give us without forming a view on what these tactics and methods might have been. But, as they could well have been a unique response to a unique set of circumstances in terms of time and space, and the scale and nature of the forces involved, it is not necessary to take a side in the lively and productive debate between the two current schools of thought on the hoplite way of war. However, two impressive manifestos, van Wees for the 'new orthodoxy' and Schwartz for the 'traditionalist' view, were particularly helpful to my visualization of the various stages of the battle.

Burn, A. R., *Persia and the Greeks: the Defense of the West 546–478 BC* Stanford CA: Stanford University Press, 1962

Cartledge, Paul, *A Sacrament in Arms: The Oath of Plataea and the End of the Persian Wars* New York: Oxford University Press, 2012

Corvisier, Jean-Nicolas, *La bataille de Platées, 479 av. J.-C.* Clermont-Ferrand: Les Editions Maison, 2010

Flower, Michael A., and Marincola, John, (ed) *Herodotus Histories Book IX* Cambridge: Cambridge University Press, 2002

Grundy, G. B., *The Battle of Plataea* London: John Murray, 1894

Hignett, C., *Xerxes' Invasion of Greece* Oxford: Oxford University Press, 1963

Krentz, Peter, *The Battle of Marathon* New Haven: Yale University Press, 2010

Lazenby, J. F., *The Defence of Greece, 490–479 BC* Warminster: Aris & Phillips, 1993

Pritchett, W. K., *The Greek State at War (volumes I–V)* Berkeley: University of California Press, 1971–91

Sabin, Philip, *Lost Battles: Reconstructing the Great Clashes of the Ancient World* London: Hambledon Continuum, 2007

Schwartz, Adam, *Reinstating the Hoplite: Arms, Armour and Phalanx Fighting in Archaic Classical Greece* Stuttgart: Franz Steiner Verlag, 2010

Snodgrass, A. M., *Arms and Armor of the Greeks* Baltimore: Johns Hopkins University Press, 1999

Shepherd, William, (trans.) *Herodotus: the Persian War* Cambridge: Cambridge University Press, 1982

Strassler, Robert B., (ed.) *The Landmark Herodotus* New York: Pantheon, 2007

van Wees, Hans, *Greek Warfare: Myths and Realities* London: Duckworth, 2004

Wright, Henry Burt, *The Campaign of Plataea* New Haven, 1904

INDEX

References to illustrations are shown in **bold**.
Plates are shown with page in **bold** and
caption in brackets, e.g. **52–53** (54).